S0-AGK-710

Working Daughter

Working Daughter

A Guide to Caring for Your Aging Parents While Making a Living

Liz O'Donnell

ROWMAN & LITTLEFIELD
Lanham • Boulder • New York • London

Published by Rowman & Littlefield
An imprint of The Rowman & Littlefield Publishing Group, Inc.
4501 Forbes Boulevard, Suite 200, Lanham, Maryland 20706
www.rowman.com

86-90 Paul Street, London EC2A 4NE

Copyright © 2019 by Liz O'Donnell
First paperback edition © 2022

All rights reserved. No part of this book may be reproduced in any form or by
any electronic or mechanical means, including information storage and retrieval
systems, without written permission from the publisher, except by a reviewer who
may quote passages in a review.

British Library Cataloguing in Publication Information Available

Library of Congress Cataloging-in-Publication Data

Names: O'Donnell, Liz (Elizabeth), author.
Title: Working daughter : how to care for your aging parents while making a living /
    Elizabeth O'Donnell.
Description: Lanham : Rowman & Littlefield, [2019] | Summary: "Working Daughter
    is the story of a woman caring for her parents while trying to hang on to her career
    and raise her kids, the lessons she learned, and the advice she has to share. This
    book provides a roadmap for women trying to navigate caring for aging parents and
    their careers. It's ideal for readers who want straight talk and real advice about the
    challenges, and the upside, to eldercare"— Provided by publisher.
Identifiers: LCCN 2018057377 (print) | LCCN 2019980329 (ebook) | ISBN
    9781538124659 (cloth) | ISBN 9781538173947 (paper) | ISBN 9781538124666
    (ebook)
Subjects: LCSH: O'Donnell, Liz (Elizabeth) | Aging parents—Care—United States.
    | Adult children of aging parents—United States. | Women caregivers—Family
    relationships—United States. | Women employees—Family relationships—United
    States. | Women caregivers—United States—Biography.
Classification: LCC HQ1063.6 .O34 2019 (print) | LCC HQ1063.6 (ebook) | DDC
    305.260973—dc23
LC record available at https://lccn.loc.gov/2018057377
LC ebook record available at https://lccn.loc.gov/2019980329

♾™ The paper used in this publication meets the minimum requirements of
American National Standard for Information Sciences—Permanence of Paper
for Printed Library Materials, ANSI/NISO Z39.48-1992.

To Bev

Contents

Acknowledgments

One day my father and I were visiting my mother at the hospice house where she spent her final months. My parents thanked me for helping them and wondered aloud how they could ever repay me. "Well since you asked," I said, "I think the least you can do is deliver me a bestseller. How about giving me your permission to share all of our dirty laundry when you're gone?" They laughed—and agreed. I am grateful to them for encouraging me in this and all of my endeavors.

I had to live this book before I wrote it and I am grateful to my family for their support throughout. Thank you to my sisters for being there when it really counts and for finding something to laugh about in every situation. Thank you to the O'Donnells, my army of love, support, and food. And most of all thank you to Kevin, Joe, and Kate for loving me.

I also want to acknowledge the working daughters and sons who shared their experiences with me and the professionals who shared advice and insight. I met so many compassionate caregivers over the last few years and I thank them for the work they do, especially Bev, the staff and volunteers at the Stanley R. Tippett Hospice Home, and the staffs at Traditions of Dedham and Charlwell House.

I am grateful to Suzanne Staszak-Silva for sharing my vision and for the team at Rowman & Littlefield for making this book a reality. I am especially grateful to Amaryah Orenstein of Go Literary—agent, editor, coach, cheerleader, guide. Thank you.

And finally, to the members of the Working Daughter community, thank you. You lift me up every day.

Introduction

He says the best way out is always through.
And I agree to that, or in so far
As that I can see no way out but through.
—Robert Frost

"The only way through is through." I co-opted the phrase from Robert Frost and made it my personal mantra back when I practiced Bikram Yoga and would struggle to hold eagle pose for thirty seconds in a 105-degree room. I used the mantra outside of the studio too, when I was trying to run three miles without stopping, or when I was struggling to complete a boring assignment at work. But I didn't fully grasp the concept until I went through hell and made it out alive.

Following a disturbing phone call from my sister on Saturday, June 14, 2014, I finally plunged head first into a role I had resisted for so long: caregiver for my elderly parents. I had been assuming more and more responsibility for them over the years—ordering their groceries online, paying their bills, hiring and managing my mother's home health aides and a visiting nurse, and accompanying them to medical appointments. I didn't do these things willingly. I wanted to help, but I didn't want to be in charge. I wasn't suited for it. I resented giving up my precious little free time to deal with what often felt to me like my parents' self-created problems. I lacked patience when Mum and Dad were disorganized or slow. I was judgmental, albeit silently, of their fridge with its expired foods, and of the increasing amounts of clutter in their spare bedroom. I was rude to the visiting nurses who didn't use email and the doctors who kept us waiting. I took my stresses out on my husband and it strained our relationship at times. And I resented my two sisters for not taking on as much as I did. In fact, just a week before the phone call that forced me into action, I had bristled at a text from my sister suggesting I join a caregiver support group "that helps people like you." People like me? Although she was probably just trying to be helpful, I took her text to mean she didn't feel a responsibility to help.

Despite my resistance, I was always there for my parents in a crisis. Anything with a clear beginning and clear end I can handle. "Contained pain" I call it, and I am good at managing it. When my mother was rushed to the hospital following a seizure, I offered to take my father to the ER because I didn't want him driving under stress. I was with him when the doctor told us my mother had a brain tumor, and my sisters and I attended every subsequent meeting with the neurosurgeon. I was twenty-three at the time. Three years later, when I was living across the country and heard my father's hand had become infected from an IV following his quadruple bypass, I called the nursing station to demand a plan and request regular updates on his progress. Eight years after that, my mother needed open-heart surgery, so I met with her surgeon, slept overnight in the SICU, and enrolled her in a cardiac rehab class post-op. When she fell and broke her nose, I picked her up out of a pool of blood, sat by her side in the ER, and moved in with her for two weeks to help her convalesce. And, a few months later, when she fell and broke her wrist but tried to hide it from me, I detected something in her voice on the phone and drove an hour and a half to meet her at the hospital.

During each crisis I would make a list of things that I should do to help my parents: hire a house cleaner, schedule appointments with specialists, look into my parents' finances, increase the hours of in-home care they received, research assisted living facilities. Then, after each dramatic event, I would allow myself a few days to take a break from daughterly duties. As I resumed my own life, those days would become weeks, and the weeks would become months. Maybe it was selfish of me to let the time pass, but I was always so busy. I am married, have two school-age children, and, at the time, I was the sole breadwinner for our family. I had a high-stress career in marketing; it was more than a job to me. And I had other responsibilities too. My elderly aunt lived a few miles away and occasionally asked for my help or ended up in the hospital herself. She had no children, so my cousins and I filled in. Outside of work and family, I had interests that took up my time. I was active in local politics, serving as a Town Meeting member and on the Warrant and Finance Committee. Publishing my first book, *Mogul, Mom & Maid* (2013), a manifesto on balancing motherhood and career, opened up opportunities for speaking engagements. I didn't want to give up any of that. "Don't I get any downtime?" "Why is it always me who has to help them?" "When do I get to have fun?" "I'd rather spend time with my kids—I barely see them as it is." "It's not fair." It's uncomfortable to admit, but that's how I felt.

Others apparently felt differently. "Caregiving is a gift." This was what people would say when I talked about my parents. And it was a common theme I'd encounter during many insomnia-induced, middle-of-the-night Google searches I conducted when I was looking for guidance. Yes, I loved my parents and it felt good to help them. But they could be difficult, and really, caregiving is a burden as much as it is a gift. Did no one else feel that way?

Mostly, I felt overwhelmed. Overwhelmed by just how much assistance my parents really needed and that I couldn't give them. Overwhelmed by how much I was already doing. Having written a book about the challenges working mothers face, I was aware of the research that said one in three mothers want to quit work after having a baby. Personally, I never wanted to quit working because of my children. But I have because of my parents. The first time I thought about quitting was when my mother's primary care doctor questioned me about why I didn't call my mother on a daily basis, why I couldn't tell him how much she ate each day, and why I hadn't moved her into my home. I'm not sure if you'd call it irony, the universe's twisted sense of humor, or mere coincidence that later that day I was going to keynote an event for new mothers and my speech was about how to balance work and family, manage competing priorities, and avoid guilt as a working mother. And here I was sitting in the doctor's office not knowing how to do any of those things as a working daughter. Maybe I shouldn't work so much, I considered. Maybe we can get by on less money. Maybe I needed to stop promoting my book. I even thought about being less present as a parent. Maybe my kids will be fine without me; they have their father and I can spend more time with them when my parents are gone.

I didn't know I wasn't alone. I hadn't yet seen the data showing that 60 percent of caregivers suffer work-related difficulties as a result of their caregiving roles[1] and that many women report changing their work arrangements to accommodate their caregiving duties by switching to a less demanding job, taking time off, or quitting altogether.[2] I didn't know I'd be one of those women, cutting my work schedule in half for several months and using up all of my vacation time to care for my parents. And I had no idea that my feelings of doubt, defeat, and guilt had barely scratched the surface and would cut so much deeper.

I was watching my son's soccer game when my sister called to tell me that my father was acting erratic and my mother didn't feel safe being alone with him. I had just returned home from two weeks of business travel and all I wanted to do was spend the weekend with my family. My kids and I were going to march in our town's Flag Day parade that night and then go to a friend's house for a cookout. As concerned as I was about what my sister told me, I was irked that my parents were in crisis, again.

My sister lives out of state, so she couldn't stay with my parents. I called my other sister who lives nearby and begged her to go. "I'll join you tomorrow," I said. "I just want tonight with my kids." I didn't care that this sister had to cancel her shift at work that night and pay more than $200 for a taxi ride to my parents' because she doesn't have a car; I was not ready to face this next crisis.

The next day, Father's Day, I packed a bag and left my husband and kids. On Tuesday, my sister and I admitted my father to the ER, and when we left he tried to escape. The ER staff gave him a powerful antipsychotic drug that rendered him helpless and incoherent, declared him harmful to himself and others, and took custody of him for seventy-two hours. On Wednesday I returned to the ER and refused to leave my father's side until I could have him transferred to a hospital of my choice. On Thursday, after he was admitted to a geriatric psych unit, I researched and toured assisted living facilities for my mother because I didn't want her home alone. On Friday, I drove more than an hour to meet with the nurses now caring for my father, and on Saturday, despite the fact my mother was complaining of stomach problems, I moved her into assisted living for a thirty-day respite stay. I walked through my own back door just after midnight on Sunday, June 22, my son's birthday; I had promised him I'd be home to celebrate. My husband and kids were asleep. I poured myself a glass of wine, sat alone in the dark, and realized there was no way out of this situation except through it.

Four hospitals, three more assisted living moves, two terminal diagnoses, and one hospice stay later, my family was out of crisis mode, and only then was I fully ready to accept my role as caregiver. I met with consultants, doctors, eldercare attorneys, and funeral directors. I sorted through powers of attorney, healthcare proxies, wills, and life insurance policies. I returned to a full-time work schedule and began traveling again for business. I attempted to balance caregiving with motherhood and career.

It wasn't an easy journey. My mother passed away four months after my sister's phone call, my father a few years after her. I cried—a lot—and had some good laughs as well. And I learned a lot too, gaining valuable insights into just what it means to be a caregiver today. I wrote this book in the hope that I could turn my family's crisis into your family's road map, so that I could pass along all of the information I gathered and the lessons I learned caring for my parents. Some names and identifying details have been changed to protect the privacy of individuals. Most importantly, I wrote this book so that some other woman doesn't find herself sitting in a gerontologist's office wondering if she should give up her job, or worse, her time with her children, because she sees no other option. And finally, I wrote this book so that you can learn not just how to survive, but how to thrive, as a caregiver.

Chapter One

Accept

"The problem is no one dies anymore."

My oldest sister looked at me, horrified by what I had said. And then she started to giggle.

"You're awful."

"It's true."

We were walking around the lake near my parents' house, the same lake we swam in as kids. It was a familiar walk, but we were in unfamiliar territory. Our father had started acting strange—he was confused by simple things, he didn't recognize his granddaughter, and he had lost all patience with our mother.

Our mother was distraught. Several years earlier, she had tripped on her Crocs, and the fall, which resulted in a broken nose, stitches, and bruising so bad she looked like her favorite flower, a pansy, had changed her. She stopped driving, started using a walker, and became housebound except for the errands, doctors' appointments, and occasional lunches out with her home health aide, a neighbor, or me.

My sisters and I saw her growing older and sadder, but we felt helpless to do anything. We wanted our parents to move to an assisted living facility, and my mother wanted that too, but my father wouldn't go. We tried to convince her to go without him—we thought they'd both be happier having their own space—but she wouldn't leave him and we didn't know how they would afford two residences anyway. Now, with my father clearly not well, my mother appeared to be at her breaking point, and my sisters and I didn't know what to do.

Most people think about the fact their parents will die someday. They prepare themselves as well as anyone can prepare for something they know nothing about. But what they don't consider—and don't prepare for—is that their parents might not die, at least not quickly or well. Parents might grow old and sick and stay that way for years; they may become frail or infirm. Nor are children ever prepared for what feels like a role reversal, when they start to care for their parents. They aren't prepared for all the times that their parents resist their support, shun their help, and ignore their advice, and they are forced to stand helplessly by and watch the people who raised and cared for them decline.

I wasn't ready for any of that. Like the time my father decided to start driving again after years of riding in the passenger seat. He was in his mid-eighties at the time and was frustrated that he couldn't take himself to the grocery store or the library.

"My brother is taking me to the RMV to renew my license," he told me.

"I hope you fail the test," I said. I knew I couldn't stop him from going, so I could only hope the trip would be fruitless.

"He'll drive whether he passes or not," my sisters warned me. They wanted me to take away his keys or remove the spark plugs from his car. Despite pressure from the two of them and many teary phone calls from my mother begging me to stop him, I didn't. He passed the test and drove himself to visit my mother, who was in a rehab facility recovering from a broken wrist. I was visiting her that day too, and he and I left together. I got in my car and watched him wander around the parking lot.

"What's up?" I yelled out my car window.

"I can't remember where I parked," he said.

"Seems to me, if you can't find your car, you shouldn't be driving it."

"Bullshit," he said. "I've been driving for over sixty years. There isn't a more qualified driver on the road."

God help us, I thought.

Nor was I prepared for what happened the night one of my cousins threw a party to celebrate the launch of my first book. I had just gotten out of the shower when my cell phone rang. It was my aunt who lived in the same town as my parents. "I don't want you to worry," she blurted out, "but your mother called us. Your father hasn't come back from his walk and he pushed his Lifeline."

The Lifeline, a pendant that both of my parents wore around their necks in case of emergency, automatically called for help in the event that someone pushed the panic button. It was dark out and my parents' neighborhood was isolated.

"Do you have his cell phone number?" my aunt asked me.

"I do. But I bet the phone is on the counter next to the toaster oven."

It was. My parents never turned it on and never carried it with them.

Part of me wasn't worried. My father frequently wandered off—not in an Alzheimer's kind of way but to visit neighbors and talk to them for hours. But part of me did start to panic. I pictured him lying beside, or in, the lake.

Fifty people were expecting me as the guest of honor in an hour but my father was missing. It would probably take me two hours to get to my parents' house on Cape Cod on a Friday night and my father could be found by then.

What was I supposed to do?

I decided I would dress for the party but pack a bag for the Cape. I'd start driving toward my cousin's house—it was in the same general direction as my parents' place—and make a decision as I drove. I tried to apply eye makeup but I had started to cry and my tears kept smudging it. Just as I was about to head out the door, my mother called.

"The jerk is alive," she sobbed. Sure enough, he had stopped to visit a neighbor and decided to demonstrate how the Lifeline worked.

And I certainly wasn't prepared to become a criminal as part of my caregiving responsibilities. But shortly after my father got back behind the wheel, he informed me that he'd climbed a ladder to clean out his gutters.

"Dad, you could fall and die," I cautioned.

"I'll take my chances" was his response.

"I'm fine with that," I said. "If you want to be a stubborn jackass and die that's your business. But if you fall and get hurt and don't die, it will be my business and I don't have time to take care of you."

He wouldn't listen. So the weekend after our phone call, I took my kids to see him. I set my alarm for early Sunday morning, snuck out of his house, carried the ladder up the street, and stashed it in the bushes behind my cousin's cottage. When he discovered it missing, my father assumed that one of the handymen my mother occasionally hired to do odd jobs stole it. The ladder is still in the bushes a few hundred feet from the house, but my parents no longer live there. And I wasn't prepared at all for how that would happen.

IT'S TIME WE GET PREPARED

In the United States, more than ten thousand people per day turn sixty-five[1] and the average expected lifespan is 78.8.[2] As a result, the number of Americans aged sixty-five and older is expected to double by the year 2050.[3] AARP predicts that by 2030, the United States will need between 5.7 and 6.6 million caregivers to support the sick and aging. That's an increase from the 1.9 million paid caregivers currently serving the elderly population in the United States.[4]

But caregiving jobs are typically low paying, physically demanding, and offer little to no healthcare benefits.[5] Couple that with the fact that the majority of services provided by home care agencies are covered by Medicare and Medicaid,[6] two organizations experiencing increasing financial pressures,[7] and industry experts do not expect we will be able to meet that demand.[8] To compensate, unpaid family caregivers will be called upon to meet the needs of older Americans. If you're not a caregiver now, chances are very good you will become one. It's high time we get prepared for the aging of America and the impact it will inevitably have on all of us.

Already, there are more than forty-four million people in the United States who provide unpaid care to an elderly or disabled person aged eighteen years or older.[9] The average caregiver is a woman in her late forties with a living parent or parents aged sixty-five or older and children she is either raising or supporting.[10] She is part of the sandwich generation, trying to balance the needs of her children with the needs of her parents—never mind her own needs. And while most caregivers are women, more and more men are taking on the role and currently represent 40 percent of all unpaid family caregivers.[11]

These caregivers hear from friends, family, so-called experts, and complete strangers how wonderful it is to be a caregiver. I heard it all the time. "What an honor it is to care for your parents," people told me. "There's no greater joy than caring for the person who once cared for you." But that wasn't how I felt.

I remember one Saturday afternoon, a week after my mother had been released from her last hospital stay, when I realized I hadn't heard from her visiting nurse even though I was told I'd get an update. I called the Visiting Nurses Association office, explained my situation, and asked that someone call me that same day as I had a lot to do and needed the update. The receptionist told me to relax. "Every day is a gift," she said.

"I see," I responded. "Do I need the gift receipt? Because I'd like to make an exchange."

Caregiving didn't feel like a gift to me. It felt like a burden—a burden I didn't want and one that I wasn't prepared to handle. I had no warning, no training, and no support. I didn't realize how many other people I knew were also caring for sick and/or elderly parents. No one in my circle of friends or coworkers was talking about it. As a working mother, I had so many people and resources to draw on for help and advice about everything from how to get a child to sleep to how to balance parenting and career. As a working daughter, I felt alone. And among the few people I knew who were family caregivers, no one was complaining about it. Just me. They must all agree it's a gift, I thought to myself. I am a horrible, selfish person for thinking it's a burden.

YOU ARE NOT ALONE

I hadn't yet met Chryssa, a sixty-year-old woman caring for her ninety-two-year-old mother and using humor to help her cope. "My mother was one of those people who every year put flowers down on her parents' graves," Chryssa told me. "I would drive her there and she'd tell me, 'When I'm dead and gone you need to do this. If you don't do it, I will haunt you.' So I told her, 'If in fact you can find a way to haunt me when you're dead, you can find a way to bring the flowers yourself.'" Her jokes bothered some people who had lost their parents, she told me. "They say, 'I would give anything if my parents were alive.' But I know they wouldn't, especially if that meant seeing their parents sick again."

I hadn't yet met Jill, whose husband whispered to me on the sidelines of our children's soccer game that sometimes Jill wished her elderly mother with cancer would just die. Nor did I have any idea my friend Cheryl's father had been diagnosed with early onset Alzheimer's and that Cheryl was a frequent caller to the Alzheimer's hotline. I had met her through a mother's group; it never occurred to us to connect as daughters.

"It feels good to be understood and know that it's okay to feel angry and frustrated when he is peeing all over the carpet and down the air vent, or shouting at me at 3 a.m.," she told me when we finally started talking about our parents. "But that's not a gift. That's kind of hellish."

I wasn't alone, I only thought I was. Of the forty-four million people doing what I was doing, 58 percent of them classified the burden of caregiving as high or moderate.[12]

Sometimes it's the small, day-to-day things that wear you down when you're a caregiver and sometimes it's the big, dramatic events. More often than not, it's a combination of both. Caregiving often creeps up on you and you don't see it coming. That's how it started for me. It began with me taking over the grocery shopping for my parents and taking my mother to her doctors' appointments—an attempt to keep my father from driving. Then my husband took over paying my parents' bills, I hired a home health aide, and then a nurse to manage their medicine. I wasn't doing a lot of physical tasks, but the constant worrying and managing wore me down. Every time my home phone rang at night or a family member would call me at the office, my chest would tighten. My mother would often say, "I don't know what I'd do without you Liz," and I would cringe. I didn't want that responsibility.

Then crisis hit. It was June 14, 2014, when my sister called and asked me to go check on our parents. Less than three weeks later, on July 1, doctors diagnosed my father with early stage Alzheimer's and dementia and told me that I had a week to move him into a memory care facility. That same day, my mother was diagnosed with ovarian cancer. She had been taken from assisted living to a local hospital just one week after she moved in. From there, she was transferred to Brigham and Women's Hospital in Boston. And it was a doctor at the Brigham who called me as I was walking out of my father's room at Quincy Hospital and told me the news. "I want to tell her tonight. What time can you get here?"

For the next few weeks my life was hell. Nights were a mix of bad dreams and insomnia. In the morning, I would experience a few seconds of peace before I opened my eyes. Then I would remember what I had to face that day and stress, anxiety, and anger would wash over me. I'd get up, brush my teeth, start a pot of coffee, and consult my Excel spreadsheet that listed everything I needed to do for my parents. At its peak, the list had 196 items.

THE JOB YOU DIDN'T APPLY FOR

That phase of intense caregiving lasted only five months, but my caregiving duties continued for years. The average duration of a caregiver's role is 4.6 years,[13] longer by one to four years for those caring for Alzheimer's and dementia patients.[14] On average, caregivers spend 24.4 hours a week providing care to their family member, although close to one-third of all caregivers provide forty-one or more hours of care a week.[15] And like me, many caregivers must find a way to fit eldercare into their already busy schedules, consumed by work and raising children.

Typical caregiving tasks vary from helping with meals and dressing or bathing to managing finances, providing transportation, and shopping.[16] In addition to helping with these daily living tasks, more than 50 percent of family caregivers are increasingly performing medical and nursing tasks such as giving injections, helping with tube feedings, and providing catheter and colostomy care.[17] These unpaid caregivers are thrust into roles that require medical, legal, and financial knowledge with very little, if any, training, and as a result find these tasks to be difficult to carry out. They need to navigate insurance policies, housing authorities, and community resources. They are required to tap into a host of softer skills like negotiation, persuasion, compassion, and patience—often while encountering and working with difficult personalities along the way. Chryssa, the sixty-year-old woman caring for her ninety-two-year-old mother, describes caregiving as "the job you didn't apply for, didn't fill out an application for, didn't train for. It's trial and error." That needs to change.

The other thing that is scarce for family caregivers is help. Just over half say another unpaid caregiver helps their care recipient and only 32 percent report help from paid caregivers.[18] It's no wonder, then, with all of the stress and responsibility, that 22 percent of caregivers think their health has deteriorated as a result of caregiving. That percent increases among people caring for someone with mental health issues or who live with the person they are caring for, are logging long hours as a caregiver, or are performing medical tasks.[19]

Employed family caregivers experience significant work-related challenges as a result of their family-related responsibilities—especially the women. While 70 percent of all working caregivers have made some job change to accommodate their caregiving role, female caregivers are more likely than males to have made alternate work arrangements such as asking for a less demanding job, taking an unpaid leave, giving up work entirely, or choosing early retirement. As a result of their reduced schedules, caregivers often suffer loss of wages and job-related benefits such as health insurance, retirement savings, and Social Security benefits. The costs are higher for women, who lose an estimated $324,044 over their lifetime due to caregiving, compared to men who lose $283,716.[20] When you consider the fact that women are projected to earn, on average, less than men due to the gender-based wage gap[21] but that they live an average of five years longer than men do,[22] it is clear that something needs to change.

This informal network of caregivers, trying to balance work, children, and aging parents, experiencing stress and career challenges, working with no support or training, is not sustainable—especially as our elderly population doubles. Especially not for women who often find their time out of the office during their childbearing years compounded by the time they take off later to care for their parents. With one in three American women already living in—or on the brink of—poverty,[23] it's imperative that we find a way to support these women, as well as the men, who are caring for their aging families. Anything less would be unfair to both the caregivers and their care recipients.

There are many ways our society can support caregivers—tax relief and training programs, better flex policies and accommodations at work, medical professionals treating caregivers as part of the care equation. Until those things happen, caregivers must advocate for themselves and prepare for their roles. And the first step in doing that is to accept it.

MOVING FROM RESISTANCE TO ACCEPTANCE

I was still resisting my role as caregiver when I walked into my mother's assisted living apartment to meet with a visiting nurse who would determine if it was time to start my mother on hospice care. "I used to be good at my job," I had written in my journal the night before. "Now I want to quit. I used to be a successful author. Now I'm irrelevant. I used to look put together. Now I am a frump." Clearly, I was in a bad place.

It didn't help my state of mind that my mother was also having a very bad day. She was in the bathroom in a state of undress when I arrived.

"What's wrong?" I asked.

"I'm just not good."

"What can I do?"

"Nothing Elizabeth," she replied, rolling her eyes.

"Jesus Christ, Mum. I'm just trying to help."

Thankfully we were interrupted by a knock on the door before our conversation got any nastier.

At first, I didn't like the hospice nurse, Peg, who entered the room like a whirlwind, carrying a roll of paper towels and laying one down under her purse and the other down on her seat. She started to explain what medications she would prescribe my mother and how I would administer them daily once I took a leave from work.

"Can I talk to you in private?" I interrupted. We went out to the seating area in the hall outside my mother's apartment and I explained to Peg that I was the sole breadwinner for my family, that I felt like I had abandoned my husband and kids six weeks earlier to deal with this crisis, that my father had been diagnosed with Alzheimer's and was adjusting to life in the memory unit downstairs, that I was using up all of my sick and vacation time to deal with the situation, that I was building a business and needed to be at work, that I couldn't do this forever, that I needed to have a life to come back to when this was all over, that I felt like my life was in shambles, and that I didn't think I wanted to work with her because I didn't like her. And then I started to sob.

Peg pulled her chair close to mine and leaned in, a gesture I would soon learn almost always signaled a compassionate but difficult conversation was about to take place. She told me not to worry about my children because I was setting an excellent example for them of unconditional love and that even though I wasn't around I was showing them I would always be there for them. Of course, that made me cry even more.

"Listen, I get it. You're the sole breadwinner. I'm a single mother of two teenage girls. I get it. We can work with you. Now, what did the doctor tell you about your mother? Ovarian cancer is a very tough cancer. We're probably looking at months."

"Okay," I said. "I can rally."

That conversation was a turning point for me. It was the moment I moved from resistance to acceptance as a caregiver. Maybe it was the fact that Peg made me feel heard that made the difference. For years, whenever anyone in the family would ask me to do something for them or ask me why I hadn't already done something they wanted me to do, they would preface it with, "I know how busy you are." Inside I would scream, "If you know how busy I am then why are you asking for my help?" The pressure I felt as a breadwinner and a mother was intense. When family made requests of my time, as innocent or necessary as those requests might have been, it felt like they weren't seeing me for who I was and what responsibilities I carried, or they weren't hearing what I was telling them—that I never had enough time with my kids, let alone any time for myself.

Peg heard me. And I knew that she did because she changed her plan right there in the hallway outside my mother's room. She let go of the idea that I would be available during the day to give my mother her pain medication and she made some calls to arrange for someone at the assisted living facility to do that. She also made it clear that there would be no judgment about my decision to keep working—from her or from me.

But ultimately, I think the reason my conversation that day with Peg changed my attitude about caregiving was that she showed me the upside. She explained what I was doing for my children—teaching them what love looked like—and for my mother—supporting her in her most vulnerable time, the end of her life. Prior to that conversation, I always looked at caregiving as something that took from me. It took away my ability to lean in at work. It took away from the time I spent with my kids and my husband. It took away my time to rest, to have fun, to be carefree, and even to be cared for. I was the rock. I was the provider. I was the adult. And I didn't like it.

Peg didn't soften the message; she didn't go easy on me. She was clear with me that my mother was going to die soon. But she was also clear that I had something to gain if I chose to accept my role. And that's what happened. I chose caregiving that day.

FROM VICTIM TO BOSS

When I made that conscious decision to choose caregiving, I took charge. I shifted my attitude from victim to boss by making caregiving work for me, not just for the people I cared for. Research suggests that "people who take an active, problem-solving approach to caregiving are less likely to feel stressed than those who worry or feel helpless."[24] Half of the caregivers surveyed by AARP and the National Alliance for Caregiving said they had no choice in taking on the responsibility to provide care for a family member. And those who felt that way reported higher stress than the caregivers who felt they had a choice. On the flip side, caregivers who feel more in control and accepting of their roles are more likely to realize positive benefits from caregiving.[25]

In the days after I met Peg, I actually took time to exercise and go on an overnight trip with my kids. I still had stress-induced bad dreams and frequent arguments with my husband, but something had shifted.

For starters, I now had a team. Until I met Peg, I felt alone as a caregiver. My sisters were trying to help but couldn't match the pace at which I felt we needed to work. My husband was frustrated by the situation I was in and expressed his displeasure. Even though he did all of the right things—cooked me meals, helped me move my parents' furniture into assisted living, figured out their finances—he said all of the wrong things, complaining about the toll my parents' crisis was taking on our family. I didn't want to hear it so I started to shut him out. But Peg was clearly on my team, and boy did I need a teammate. She managed the logistics of ordering and delivering medication for my mother. She coached me on what to say to the health insurance company. And she checked in on me to make sure I was eating, sleeping, and taking care of myself. And the more I leaned on Peg, the more comfortable I got asking for and accepting help from others.

I also had a plan. Before I accepted my role as caregiver, I had a to-do list, but that's not the same thing. I didn't know what would happen as the cancer progressed. Now I knew who would help, where my mother would stay, and what my role would be as she approached her death. Accepting my role, taking charge of the experience, and creating a plan all put me in a position to access the upside of caregiving—and there is an upside.

ACCESSING THE CAREGIVER'S GAIN

There is a growing body of research about something called "the caregiver's gain," but outside of hollow statements from well-meaning friends and family that caregivers are "blessed to be able help a loved one," the upside of caregiving has received far less attention than the downside. A 2006 study in *The Gerontologist*, a journal published by the Gerontological Society of America, stated caregiving "increased [caregivers] feelings of pride in their ability to meet challenges, improved their sense of self-worth, led to greater closeness in relationships, and provided an enhanced sense of meaning, warmth, and pleasure."[26] And, in a 2011 article titled "Caregiving's Hidden Benefits," *The New York Times* cited research conducted by Dr. Lisa Fredman, an epidemiologist at Boston University, who found that caregivers had "lower mortality rates than noncaregivers, maintained stronger physical performance than non-caregivers, and did significantly better on memory tests."[27] More recently, Fredman teamed up with Dr. David L. Roth of John Hopkins University and Dr. William E. Haley of the University of South Florida and reported that, even though caregiving can be stressful and burdensome, most caregivers also experience personal benefits from assisting loved ones.

> Many caregivers experience both positive experiences and some strain simultaneously. To be connected through caring relationships with other human beings, especially within one's own family, is a common human experience that is desired by virtually everyone. Providing care for an older family member or friend with a chronic illness or disability is an increasingly common and important type of caring relationship. We assert that the "caregiving-is-stressful" assumption is an overly narrow, simplified, and limited view on these types of human relationships.[28]

KEEP CHOOSING

After my mother passed away, I continued to choose caregiving. I found support. I found a great primary doctor for my father, one who listened to me. I worked closely to coordinate my father's care with the staff at his senior residence. I kept my husband in the loop on what was going on with my father—it turns out he was more willing to help me and accept his role as my support team when I kept him informed. And I created timelines that allowed me to focus and not get too overwhelmed. For example, after my mother died in late October 2014, I gave myself until the end of the year just to accept the loss. In January, realizing how much I still had to do to wrap up her affairs—insurance claims, bank accounts, cleaning out her belongings—I gave myself until June 14, the anniversary of the original crisis, to work through the logistics. When June 14 came, I told myself I was in a new phase of caring for an elderly parent, that I needed to focus on how things were in that moment and not worry about what caregiving would look like as my father got sicker or weaker. But I developed a plan for if—or when—that happened. I made sure to know how much money my father had and what he could afford. I knew who I would call if I needed help. I developed a routine for visiting him and running his errands.

If you are resisting your role as caregiver, I urge you to step in and get on with it. It won't be easy, but it's most likely inevitable. Right after my mother died, I ran into a woman I knew who told me that her elderly father, the primary caregiver to her wheelchair-bound mother, was very sick and was resisting her offers to help. This woman is incredibly competent and it was obvious she cared about her parents even though she described them as difficult. "But I give up," she said. "If he doesn't want my help, I'm not going to force him."

I remember thinking to myself, "You should tell her to just do it. Tell her to help them despite their resistance because eventually it will get worse." But just weeks after burying my mother, I wasn't feeling strong enough to give anyone else advice. I wish I had been. Nine months later, I ran into this woman again and she told me her father's health had deteriorated even more and that she and her siblings were scrambling to find a facility for both of their parents. The only way through is through.

To be clear, I am not advocating for you to be a people-pleasing doormat. The most important thing you can do as a caregiver is to do it on your own terms. I'm suggesting that if you are going to take on the role, own your choice. Acceptance will put you in a much better position to access the caregiver's gain.

Here are two tools to help you on your path to acceptance.

Begin with the end in mind.

This is one of Stephen Covey's "Seven Habits of Highly Successful People." When I began my caregiving journey, I didn't know there was something called the caregiver's gain. I only knew about the burden and the stress. You, however, have been informed. Think about the good that can come from your decision to be a caregiver. Visualize how you will feel after caring for someone in his or her most vulnerable moments. Think about the possibility of building a relationship with your family member based solely on being present, not on emotions or past history. Think about how satisfying it is to do something because it's what you want to do, not because anyone else is telling you that you should or because you are expecting external rewards or gratification. These are some of the intangible benefits of caregiving if you choose to access them.

Speak your truth.

You don't need to be a Pollyanna about caregiving. You do not need to pretend that caregiving is wonderful. Sometimes it sucks. So go ahead and complain. Be honest. If I hadn't been honest with Peg that I had doubts and limitations and didn't even like her at first, I probably wouldn't have found the right support because she wouldn't have known what I needed.

Try this: Set two timers every morning, each for one minute. For the first minute complain, wail, sob, or whine. If you need the time to express your stress, take it. Then move on. Set a second timer, again for one minute. Spend that minute listing all of the things for which you are grateful. It could be big things like your health or your children or small things like chocolate and wine. During the darker moments of caregiving, you can call up this list to remind you all is not horrible. When the timers go off, move forward with your day. After all, there is care to be given.

Chapter Two

Absolve

"Elizabeth, I don't want to see your father again."

My eighty-four-year-old mother told me this a few days after I moved my father to a memory care facility. For years I had suggested my parents live apart because I thought they'd be happier doing their own thing. But *now*? My father had been diagnosed with Alzheimer's and dementia and was locked up against his will and *now* I was supposed to tell him he would never see his wife again? I was so angry with my mother.

I wanted to tell her to do it herself, or better yet not at all, but she had just been diagnosed with ovarian cancer and was given three months to live. I couldn't really express my feelings to her now. Wasn't it supposed to be all about her and what she wanted from now on? But what about him? And what about me?

My parents had already been apart for the three weeks since I admitted my father to the ER. My mother kept telling me she felt guilty about my father's hospitalization and subsequent move to the memory facility because it was her phone call to my sister that started this chain of events. But I felt guilty too. I was the one who convinced him he should go to the ER. My sister and I were the ones who took him to Dairy Queen for an ice cream and then drove him to the hospital. We were the ones who left him there over-night, only to return the next day and find him restrained (he was strapped to a gurney), speaking gibberish, unaware of where he was, what year it was, or who we were, and barely able to walk on his own. I thought the father I had always known was gone forever and that I was the one who killed him.

Because he needed to be hospitalized and because we didn't know what was wrong and if or when he would return home, my sisters and I decided to send my mother to a local assisted living facility, just for thirty days, so we could figure things out. My mother was scared and frail. She no longer drove and we didn't want her at home alone. We needed to go to work, so staying with her wasn't an option.

A few months earlier, I had started a new job building the Boston office of a California-based public relation firm. It was both a blessing and a curse that I worked three thousand miles away from my boss and all of my coworkers. On the one hand, I could rush to my parents' house in an emergency. As long as I was responsive to my clients and got my work done, no one noticed if I was in the office or not. But on the other hand, I had no local support. Plus, building a business wasn't a nine-to-five gig. I needed to be out in the community networking, interviewing candidates, and looking for clients.

I knew my mother was nervous about the temporary move, but she agreed that we couldn't continue to stay with her. I could only imagine how overwhelming it must have been for her, sweet but shy, to leave her home and go to a place where she didn't know the staff, where she didn't know the residents, and where she had to eat her meals in a dining room full of strangers every day. And I knew she wasn't feeling well either. So I tried to shield her from what was going on with my father. I gave her vague updates, telling her he was acting confused and forgetful and that maybe the urinary tract infection the hospital staff had diagnosed was to blame. I tried to be patient with her but her proclamations of guilt irritated me; I didn't have time to comfort her because I was so worried about my father.

Perhaps my relationship with my father should have been complicated, but it wasn't. My father had a short fuse and a quick temper and he yelled once a day, his volume way out of proportion to the infractions that upset him. He'd yell because the flowers in his garden needed to be weeded or watered, a chore he assigned to his daughters, or because someone had emptied the ice trays and not refilled them or hadn't brought the ash barrels, as he still called them, up the driveway after the garbage collectors emptied them. As a defense, I tried to be a very good daughter and never disappoint him.

As a teenager and a young adult, I couldn't get enough time with my father. He was curious and smart, which meant we could talk for hours about anything. When I started playing the flute, we talked about music. He loved Ravel and Stravinsky, and introduced me to his friend who had gone to Julliard. When I joined the marching band and went to band camp, he told me stories about marching in step with his Army troop for miles on end, in the heat, carrying a heavy pack on his back. He came to every show and competition and he was the sole audience member when the high school band performed at the opening of the local Ames department store. And when I started working in the technology industry, he learned everything he could about personal computing.

As I got older, I became less tolerant of his shortcomings. I had no problem telling him to shut up and grow up when he ranted about something insignificant. He didn't always listen, but I didn't hold back. The lines of communication between us were wide open. I didn't always understand my father. I didn't always like my father. But I always loved him and he knew it.

And so when my father was transferred to Quincy Hospital, I showed up in warrior mode. I met every nurse, doctor, and attendant who was going to care for him and told them I wanted them to call me any time, day or night, if he needed me. I told every single one of them that the condition my father arrived in was not his baseline behavior. When one of the nurses, Josh, pointed out that I had already given him that information, I told him, "Yes, I know I told you. And I know you heard me. But I didn't know if you really listened."

I stayed by my father's side all day. At one point that first night he woke up and wanted to talk.

"I have three daughters," he told me. "Their names are Rita, Eileen, and, and, hmmm I can't think of it. Their names are Rita, Eileen, and . . . it will come to me. Hang on. Oh hell, I don't remember," he said.

"Are you kidding me?" I asked him. He may have been sicker than I had ever seen him, but I was not letting him off the hook. "Liz, Dad! Her name is Liz, and it's me, the one sitting here at 11 o'clock at night. I don't see the others here."

He started to laugh. I had always fancied myself his favorite child, although he never said that was the case. So much for that theory.

That same night, I drove back to Cape Cod so that I could take my mother to respite care the following morning. She wasn't feeling well so she asked if we could both stay in the guest room. We slept beside each other in the twin Hitchcock beds with gold acorns stenciled on the headboards that came from the childhood bedroom I had shared with my middle sister. My mother was hot and dizzy and felt nauseous. I was worried about my father, tired, and cranky.

In the middle of the night my mother had what must have been a panic attack. She was gasping for air, sweating, and felt faint. I thought I should take her to the ER but instead I sent a text to my sister in Ohio. *Mum dry heaves shivers hot what the hell do I do*, and then, *I can't go through this (ER) 2x in one week. I am fried!!!!!*

We made it through the night, and in the morning I got a call from nurse Josh, who told me my father had had a good morning. My mother did not. She got sick and I had to clean her, something I wasn't prepared to do.

When I finished, I ran outside, gasping for fresh air and gagging. When I came back in she said to me, "You're just like your father."

It was 4 o'clock in the afternoon by the time we got to the assisted living place, and while we were sitting in the director's office filling out paperwork, I got another call from Quincy Hospital. The night nurse asked me if I could talk to my father. He was refusing to take his medicine and she hoped I could calm him down and convince him to comply.

"Liz, call the police," my father said. "I've been kidnapped."

"Dad, you are in the hospital and I need you to take your medicine. If you do, I promise I will come see you tonight."

I couldn't wait to get back to Quincy to reassure my father he was in a safe place, but I couldn't just leave my mother at the door of the assisted living home. I had to at least stay for dinner and unpack her suitcase. I felt guilty leaving her there and I felt guilty that I didn't get back to the hospital until 11 p.m. I felt even more guilty that I wouldn't see either of my parents the next day because I had promised my kids a trip to New York City for their birthdays and, even though I no longer wanted to go, I didn't want to disappoint them.

The trip was not a vacation, not for me anyway. I was glued to my cell phone in the taxi to and from the Staten Island Ferry, trying to get work done. Even though I had scheduled time off from work, I was behind on some projects from the week prior. My client was launching a new website and I had to proof all of the copy. While my husband and kids were taking in the sights, I was reading and sending emails.

And the next day, in the middle of Times Square, my family witnessed a bike messenger get hit by a taxi. My husband ran into the street to help while I called 911. As I was dialing my phone, my hands trembling, the assisted living home called to inform me that my mother had been sent to the hospital with severe stomach pains.

A few days later, on July 1, 2014, my sister and I met with my father's medical team and they told us he had early stage Alzheimer's and dementia and could never go home. A few hours later, a doctor from Boston's Brigham and Women's Hospital called my cell phone. My mother had been transferred there the day before.

"Liz, your mother has ovarian cancer." He predicted that she had three months to live.

Like some kind of wind-up toy, I powered through the following days and weeks. I went to my parents' house to find information on their insurance policies, pension plans, and wills. I had my father deemed incompetent and met with a lawyer to become his power of attorney. I spent hours on the phone with my cousins who were nurses to discuss the diagnoses, my cousin the social worker to discuss care facilities, and I asked my other cousins, who were on vacation on the Cape, if they would take my kids to the beach. I went to my office and pretended to work, and I toured memory care facilities for my father and assisted living facilities for my mother. Because my mother had opted out of treatment, the hospital had discharged her immediately and without warning. Without a plan, I had sent her back to the respite care facility—after all, we had prepaid for the month—but I wanted to move her closer to me.

In the end, I found a place less than two miles from my house that had both a memory care unit and assisted living, and I signed a lease for each of my parents. I thought it would be easiest on me to have them close by and under one roof. And then my mother told me she was leaving my father.

My relationship with my mother was complicated. Maybe that's just how it is between mothers and daughters. Years earlier, after my mother had heart surgery, I was staying with my parents to help out and my mother was getting flustered, trying to sort the fourteen different pills she had been prescribed. My father got frustrated watching her and in his own high-volume way tried to help. She didn't want his help and so she went into her bedroom to get away from him. I proceeded to tell him he was an insensitive jerk and I went into the guest room to get away from him. A few hours later, I went to the kitchen to get a glass of water. My father was sitting there watching *Law & Order*, or maybe the 11 o'clock news. My mother came out to get her pre-bedtime bowl of ice cream and gave my father a big hug.

"Good night. I love you," she said.

I was furious with her. Why the hell was I giving him the silent treatment if she wasn't even angry anymore?

And so when my mother told me she didn't want to see my father, perhaps I should have applauded her act of independence. But my first thought was, "Why should I have to tell him what you think, when you never did?" My second thought was, "What the hell am I going to do about their living arrangements?"

I met with the assistant director at the senior living facility and told her my dilemma, and she assured me we could make it work. She would let the staff know the situation and said my parents wouldn't run into each other because my father was locked in a different section. The only thing we had to figure out, she told me, was who would go to the luau. Apparently, every summer they hosted a big Hawaiian-themed party for all of the residents, including the dementia patients and their families.

I had no other options and so I moved them both in, terrified it wouldn't work out. The night I got home from moving my mother in, I received a text from my sister in Ohio. *Did Mum move? How is she? How is Dad? How are you?*

I added a subject to the verb "move" and replied: *I moved Mum.*

I had so much resentment toward my sisters. I was handling so much— medication, daily visits, moving—and my life was falling apart. I wasn't sleeping. I had no clean laundry. My husband and I were arguing, and I was behind at work. They, on the other hand, seemed to be going about their daily routines. I could feel the anger rising in my chest, and so of course I picked a fight with my husband. Then I made a list in my journal of all the people I was mad at. It included my sisters, my husband, strangers who said hello to me when I didn't have the energy to respond, and "my parents for their fucked-up marriage that led to their separate living arrangements and the lies and secrets and accompanying stress."

I spent that weekend shuffling back and forth between their two rooms. It was so much easier having them in the same facility, except for the sneaking around. After every visit my mother would wave goodbye to me from her apartment window, so I had to get in my car and drive away and then drive back and go through the back door to visit my father. But that didn't last long because two days later the assistant director told me one of the staff members had invited my mother to the luau. I had to tell them the truth.

A few days earlier, I had met with the head of gynecological oncology at one of the top hospitals in Boston. He was a colleague of my cousin and met me as a favor to her. I had intended to talk to him about my mother's medical prognosis but instead I blurted out that she wanted to leave my father after fifty-two years of marriage and with only three months to live.

"You need to honor your mother's decisions," he told me, and said he'd seen that behavior before. "People facing death can get really clear about their legacy and we have to respect that."

I tried to keep his words in mind when I told my mother that my father was living a floor below her. But when she told me not to tell him she had cancer, I got angry. I didn't say anything because I was ashamed of what I was thinking. I felt like she was leaving me to bear the brunt of my father's heartbreak when he eventually learned the whole story. Why should it be me left holding the bag? And, I wondered, whose cancer was this anyway? My mother was the one getting all of the attention, but I was the one whose life was in turmoil. Sure, her life was ending, but she was eighty-four. How tragic was that? My life seemed to be ending too, and I was supposed to have years ahead of me. Wasn't that the real tragedy?

"You must be tired," she said in response to my silence.

"Not really," I said, and I left.

Walking to the parking lot, I looked up to see my mother in the window, holding a stuffed animal my niece had bought for her and waving goodnight to me. In that moment, I just wanted to hug her.

DUSTING OFF DYSFUNCTION

When we take on the role of caregiver for one or both of our parents, old family dynamics and dysfunction will inevitably surface. The task before us requires us to be adults, but suddenly we feel like our nine-year-old selves again. Memories are triggered and our buttons pushed. It can be disorienting and overwhelming. One minute we think we've become the parent, and we want to tell our parents what to do. The next minute we are the children, and we want to be comforted by the people we are supposed to be comforting.

And if our childhood was difficult, or worse, dangerous, those feelings can resurface and make us feel unsafe again.

In the online support group I run for working daughters, I see as many posts about the tactical challenges of caregiving—administering medications, scheduling home health aides, managing finances—as I do the emotional challenges—unappreciative or unkind parents, unhelpful siblings, and opinionated relatives.

Nicole became estranged from her father, whom she described as a "phenomenal surgeon but a tough character," in her early twenties. At the age of fifty, she ran into him at a family birthday party.

"He was homeless. He was living in a car, a hoarder. Dire straits for someone who had been a surgeon."

Her father had Alzheimer's.

Nicole "adopted" him that day and brought him home to live with her and her teenage son. Between his personality and the effects of the disease, her father went through what she describes as "ugly phases" and was violent at times. Nicole's son decided to go to boarding school to get out of the house. Nicole's friends stopped calling, her social life dwindled, and her aunts and brother questioned her motivation in taking her father in. Because she was no longer able to attend professional networking events, the consulting projects she did for startup companies started to dry up, as did her income. And yet Nicole doesn't regret her decision.

"I made a choice, and I am compromising my career. I am changing my son's life. But my father is a human being going through a really difficult thing and I know how to take care of someone. I am going to keep him out of harm's way. And if someday I have to take care of my brother, I will."

Nicole found a way to be at peace with her father and her role as his caregiver. She did that by setting really clear boundaries about what she would tolerate, what she was willing to give up, and what she thought she was gaining. She still managed to consult on a few projects, but eventually she shifted from marketing startups to investing in them with some family resources she was lucky to access. Perhaps most importantly, she found the good in her situation.

WHAT'S GOOD?

Every Thursday I ask the working daughters in my online support group "What's good?" because I believe there is something good in every situation; sometimes we just need to search for it. I didn't always feel that way, but in the summer of 2014, I needed to find something positive to focus on. My thoughts were so negative and I was worried they were making me sick.

I walked around thinking, "Woe is me," "Why me?" and "Poor me." I was fixated on the idea that it was so unfair for the youngest daughter to be her parents' caregiver, handling more than her sisters. I felt like a victim.

So I decided I had to find something good about my situation and I searched for another angle. Yes, I was doing the majority of the caregiving for my parents, but that was because I was able to. The flip side of feeling like a victim was recognizing that I had the competence, the organizational skills, and the energy to do what needed to be done. And that felt good.

THE FOUR TRAPS OF
CAREGIVING WITH SIBLINGS

In changing my perspective, I was able to avoid one of the four common traps of caregiving with siblings: resentment. The other three are:

Wishful Thinking

"Why don't you have one of your sisters do that?" my husband would often ask when I was doing something for my parents. I understood where he was coming from, but I also knew he was practicing wishful thinking. We all have different strengths and weaknesses. I am great at execution and can manage logistics like nobody's business. Couple that with my assertiveness and I am often the best person to ask questions of oncologists, negotiate assisted living leases, or lead meetings with the eldercare attorney.

I'm not so good when it comes to the emotional tasks or the soft skills. My sisters are much, much better in those areas than I am. So it would have been wishful thinking to ask them to take on some of my tasks and expect they would handle them the way I would. Better for me to ask them to step in where I wasn't very good.

Indecision

If you are "the one," chances are you are, or will be, your parents' power of attorney and healthcare proxy. If that is the case, you are in charge. Own it. It's good practice to ask for input from your siblings but know when to stop gathering opinions and take action. Your parents gave you the role because they trusted you. You need to trust yourself. If your siblings don't like it, that is unfortunate. But you are not caring for them.

One way to avoid indecision while also avoiding alienating family members is to take a high input low democracy approach, a concept I learned from my boss. Get everyone's feedback. Value it. Weigh it. And then make your best decision. Hopefully, your family will understand if your decision isn't in line with their input. And if they don't, just know you listened and acted to the best of your ability.

Indiscretion

As a caregiver, you will most likely spend plenty of time with your aging or ailing parent. And during those interactions you may be tired, stressed, and frustrated with your siblings. Don't mention it! Find a friend, a spouse, or an online support group to vent to. Do not unload on the person who requires care. They have enough to worry about and do not need the guilt, worry, and stress that come from knowing family rifts are forming.

About a week before my mother died, one of the last times she was awake, she took my hand and said, "Promise me you will be good to your sisters."

"Damn it, I was trying to avoid this moment," I joked. "But of course I will Mum."

It was what she needed to hear. And I meant it.

Of course, sometimes we need a professional to help us sort through complex family relationships and feelings. Therapy was high on my wish list when my parents got sick, and I'm sure my sisters would have loved for me to go too, but due to time and financial constraints, I couldn't make it work. Between caring for my parents, being available for my own family, and juggling my work obligations, I had to find a way to deal with my feelings on my own. And while not all wounds can be healed, it is possible to find a way to work within existing family dynamics and avoid new family drama in order to minimize the stresses of caregiving.

SIX QUESTIONS TO ASSIST
YOU IN SETTING BOUNDARIES

If you are struggling with feelings of anger, frustration, or guilt, answering the following questions will help you set the personal boundaries you need to protect yourself while caring for someone else.

1. Is what I am feeling in the present or from the past?

If the feelings that have surfaced for you are from the past, is it possible for you to release them? Can you be open to creating a new relationship based on who and where you are today? Ask yourself: Do these feelings serve any purpose for me now?

2. Am I able to forgive?

If you are harboring anger or hurt from a past or recent infraction, can you forgive? Can you accept that the person who hurt you was doing the best they could or that they are sorry for their behavior?

3. Is this the right time to resolve an issue?

Maybe now isn't the time to delve into past problems or hurt feelings. Do not work out sibling rivalries, for example, in front of a sick parent or during a crisis situation. Save it for another time. But if your issue is with your parent, and he or she has limited time left, do try to find a peaceful resolution to past issues. A hospital or hospice social worker can help.

4. What behaviors from others am I willing to tolerate?

Can you care for someone who doesn't say thank you or doesn't respect your time? There is no right answer. The important thing is to think about it and decide what is right for you.

5. What am I able and willing to handle right now?

You get to choose how much you take on. It may not feel that way, but it is true. I chose to take on the logistics of caring for my parents and I asked my out-of-state sister to be the one who called and talked to them every night. I was not willing to do both.

6. What am I willing to give?

Just because you are able to do something doesn't mean you have to. If you are going to be a compassionate caregiver, you must offer care on your own terms. I was willing to lose sleep and miss some of my children's soccer games, but I was not willing to lose my job as a result of my parents' illnesses. If you don't think you can care for someone without harming yourself emotionally or physically, you don't have to.

DUTIFUL DAUGHTER DISEASE

I mentioned that as a child, I always tried to be a good daughter. It's a role many women cast themselves in—that of the good girl. We aim to please—first our parents, then our teachers, our spouses, our children, and eventually our parents again. By casting ourselves in that role over and over, we begin to believe that's what others expect of us. But there are no gold stars for perfect behavior. In fact, there is no perfect in caregiving. The best we can do is the best we can do.

Notice if you are acting from a desire to be a people pleaser; it's the fastest path to resentment and it will block you from establishing a healthy relationship with your family members. If you are suffering from dutiful daughter disease, go buy yourself a small mirror to keep in your purse. Make looking in that mirror the first and last thing you do every day. In the morning, remind yourself that the person looking back at you is the only person whose approval you need. At night, make eye contact and ask yourself if you did the best you could. Right there, in that mirror, is your most important relationship.

THE DOs AND DON'Ts OF MANAGING GUILT

Be prepared to feel guilty when you start setting boundaries. Caregiver guilt runs the gamut from thinking your actions hurt someone (I didn't visit therefore my parents were lonely) to wishing you did something but didn't (I wanted to call yesterday but I didn't), guilt that you didn't do enough (I should have worked late because everybody else was), and even guilt for what you are thinking (I can't take this anymore!).

To help manage your guilt, check your feelings of omnipotence. Guilt makes you think you have more power than you do. You do not. You are also not responsible for other people's feelings. Behavior experts call this disproportionate guilt. It makes you feel responsible for things you have no control over—like other people's lives.

Follow these four tips for managing guilt.

Do practice forgiveness.

Why are you beating yourself up for not visiting your father this weekend? If you didn't see him because you were busy running the kids to soccer games and birthday parties and being a good parent, that's forgivable, isn't it? If you didn't visit him because you were exhausted after a trying and stressful week at work or you were working two shifts to feed your family and you needed some time to rest and recuperate, that's forgivable, isn't it? If you didn't visit him because sometimes it's just too hard to deal with his dementia or grumpy disposition and you are just human after all, that's forgivable, isn't it? I'll answer for you. It is.

Do establish priorities.

Guess what? You probably can't give everything your all. So you need to make some choices. Where are you going to crush it and where are you going to cruise? When my parents were diagnosed with their respective illnesses, my boss suggested I take a leave of absence so that I could be available to them; I was afraid she would say that. While I understood her perspective—she needed to know I could be counted on to perform if I were on the payroll—I couldn't afford not to earn my full paycheck. We agreed I would work a few hours a day and use up my sick and vacation time to cover the hours I took off, and I assured her my work would not suffer. Of course it did, and I had to accept that my end-of-year performance evaluation would be the first time since I graduated college that I didn't get rave reviews. Rather than beating myself up and feeling guilty that I hadn't met all of my performance goals, I reminded myself constantly that my most important work was the work I was doing outside of the office for my family. My bonus that year was the satisfaction I felt from steering my family through crisis. And like all crises, it would end one way or another and I could turn back to my work again with full commitment.

Working daughters ask me all of the time if they should tell their managers about their eldercare responsibilities, and my answer is always "It depends." In chapter 4 I outline some scenarios for when sharing is a good idea and when it is not. But in general, if you feel secure in your job, it's a good idea to let your boss know that you are managing a situation at home and there may be times you will have to deal with it during work hours. Ask him or her how he or she would like you to handle those situations if they arise. The answer will help you prioritize. Plus, being transparent will assuage any guilt you may be feeling about your personal life impacting your professional one.

Don't think you can control the situation.

If there is one thing caregiving teaches us, it is that we are not in control. We can't control illness. We can't control death. We can't control how our siblings behave or how our parents feel. And no, despite how much I try, we can't control whether or not the doctor is running late. Therefore we can't take responsibility for any of those things. The sooner we understand that, the sooner we can manage some of that caregiver guilt.

Don't try to be perfect.

Perfection is highly overrated. When we strive to be the perfect daughter, the perfect worker, or the perfect wife and mother, we are setting ourselves up to fail because too much in life is out of our control. And you know what? No one except for you expects you to be perfect. Let it go.

THE WORST WORD FOR CAREGIVERS

If you are going to be truly effective in managing tough relationships, there is one word I urge you to remove from your vocabulary. It's the word "should." Whenever you start a sentence or a thought with "I should," that is an indicator that you have internalized someone else's expectations and values. I should call my mother. I should visit more often. I should be able to handle all of this.

Take a few minutes and listen to the "shoulds" in your head. As a caregiver, your head is probably full of them. Are you surprised at how many there are? How many of those shoulds are your own voice and how many are based on someone else's value system playing in your head? Chances are your shoulds come from other people: your parents, siblings, extended family, professional caregivers, doctors, so-called experts, the media. You should move your father into your home. You should take time off of work to help your parents. You should call/visit/help more. When you act on shoulds instead of on your own wants, you grow resentful—and fast. At the end of the day, the only opinion that really matters is the one you have of yourself. Only you know the circumstances, the time constraints, the resources, and the relationships that impact you as a caregiver. Others may judge, but that's not your issue.

Try this exercise to erase the shoulds from your mind: Get a piece of paper and fold it into two columns. In the left column, list all of the shoulds playing in your head. Then in the right column, list the things you truly want to do as a caregiver. Don't worry about how you will accomplish those things or what the outcome will look like, just list them. Don't think about this exercise too much, just start writing.

When you have exhausted the lists, look for the relationships between the should and the wants. In the lefthand column may be something like, "I should visit my Mom daily and help her so she can remain in her home." That "should" may have a match on the right that looks like this: "I want to help my mother live as independently as possible." Now think about where you truly must step in and make that want happen. Do you really need to take over running your mother's household in order for her to stay at home? Of course not. Perhaps siblings can help. Perhaps a home health aid is an option. Maybe your mother just needs to retrofit the house. Maybe she just needs rides to appointments or meals delivered a few days a week. See? You are not all powerful in your mother's life. She and you have many options. Act on what you want to do to help, not what you think you should do.

When my mother stopped driving, I felt like I should take her grocery shopping every weekend. I felt like that was what my relatives thought a good daughter would do. But I worked all week and only had forty-eight brief hours each weekend to rest, spend time with my husband and children, run my own errands—live my life. But because I listened to the "shoulds" in my head, I drove three hours round trip every weekend to take my mother to the grocery store. The trip to the store took forever—my mother used a walker by that time—and I always rushed home as soon as the groceries were put away. And I was cranky. I was cranky while I was with my mother. I was cranky at home with my husband. I was cranky with my kids because I felt squeezed for time. Nobody won. And then one day, it just clicked. I wanted to get groceries for my mother. I did not want to take her to the store. I was willing to order the food online or do the shopping by myself because it was faster. And I wasn't all powerful in my mother's life. If she didn't like what I was willing to offer, she had other options. And so I started ordering the groceries online and visiting with her on the weekends. My mother missed her trips to the store, but sometimes a neighbor would take her, she always had food, and I had more time to sit and visit with her.

Here's another example. In the should column you may have written something like, "I should accompany my father to all of his doctor's appointments." The match in the want column might say, "I want to be my father's healthcare proxy and advocate." There are ways to achieve what you want without spending several hours a month, or a week, in waiting rooms. You can schedule consultations with the doctor. You can email the doctor questions. You can be a powerful and effective proxy without taking time off of work or away from your kids.

REDEFINING RELATIONSHIPS

Another option for building healthier relationships with your parents is to redefine and restructure your relationship with them. Nowhere is it written that you can't change the dynamic. Caregivers often talk about the role reversal they experience when they start taking care of their parents. Suddenly they feel like they are the parent, worrying about their parents' well-being, maybe supporting them financially, or feeding and bathing them. But maybe there's another alternative—one you haven't explored yet, one that isn't centered on parent-child dynamics. What if you open yourself up to the possibility that in your caregiving role, you can create a brand new relationship with your aging parent—one that isn't tied to the past and that is based on two adults working together?

Sadly, my mother didn't stay in the assisted living facility very long. After only two weeks, we transferred her to a hospice home because she needed 'round-the-clock care. Once that happened, my role with her switched back from caretaker to daughter. There was not much left for me to do for her—just sit with her and soak up our remaining time together. With no agenda and no to-do list, I learned to enjoy just being with her—no expectations, no baggage. The past and the future didn't matter; we merely connected in the moment.

And then one day she asked me to bring my father to see her. I was thrilled. She told him how she felt about him. She told him that she forgave him.

"Come visit me anytime," she said to him.

When I was leaving to take my father back to memory care, I leaned over to kiss her goodbye and I whispered in her ear, "I am so proud of you Mum." But it was more than pride that I felt. It was admiration.

Chapter Three

Prioritize

"I don't know what's going to last longer," I told a friend in the fall of 2014. "My mother or my marriage." My mother had been in a hospice home for two months and I visited her every day. Some days I stopped there on my way to my office and then worked late to make up the time. Some days I went after dinner and watched *Criminal Minds* reruns with her from 7 o'clock until almost midnight.

Ever since my sister called me to tell me something was wrong with my parents, I had left my husband to do all of the parenting of our two kids. He did it without complaining, but I wanted more from him. I wrote in my journal one night, "I just want to be treated with kid gloves but that's not who I married."

I was bitter, or envious, or both because he seemed to be unaffected by what was happening to my parents and was living our normal life—school, soccer, homework—while my life had been hijacked by cancer and Alzheimer's. And because I had dropped everything to run to my parents' aid, as I had many times before, he was a little bitter too.

My marriage was tense through the summer and fall of 2014, and it certainly didn't help when one of my cousins, who was my rock through all of my caregiving crises, told me, "The most helpful thing for me, when my parents were sick, was coming home to my husband's embrace every night." Really? Most of the conversations I was having with my husband at the time ended with a four-letter word followed by "you." In fact, one day when I was at work, I got a text from him commenting on how I had incorrectly put my breakfast dishes in the dishwasher. I replied: *My mother is dying and I'm managing the whole fucking process I don't give a goddamn motherfucking flying piece of shit about how to stack the dishwasher.*

Just as my mother got clear about her priorities when she was given her cancer diagnosis, I did too after talking to Peg the hospice nurse, who had told me that work and children would still be there when my mother was gone. But I made my choice to put my parents ahead of all else without consulting my husband. I just expected him to understand. And it was clear he did on one level because he helped me with the hundreds of tasks I had to handle. He rented a U-Haul to move my mother's furniture into the assisted living facility and, a few weeks later, he rented another one and moved the furniture back to Cape Cod when she transferred to hospice. He sorted through my parents' finances and handled their medical bills and insurance claims. But on another level, he didn't understand at all.

One night while my mother and I were watching TV, one of the hospice nurses came into the room and whispered in my ear, "One of our patients passed away. I am going to shut the door so your mother doesn't hear the body being taken out."

Eventually I came to recognize the sound that the wheels of a funeral director's gurney make, but that night—the first time I was in such close proximity to death—I was shaken up. And then I got a text from my husband telling me he would "wait up" for me because I was going away for a few days to San Francisco for work. Great. I could just imagine his reaction when I got home and told him I wasn't in the mood. "Once again, she put her parents first."

But how could he really understand what I was going through? No one can unless they have been a caregiver too. That's probably why 80 percent of people caring for an aging parent say caregiving puts a strain on their relationship or marriage and 34 percent say it has a negative impact on their sex life.[1] Perhaps we caregivers should make our partners a list of things that make us not in the mood. It could include disease, dying, death, dementia, and Depends. And when we have our choice between sleep and, well, anything else, we're going to choose sleep.

Yes, eldercare has the potential to really disrupt our lives. And it's not just our spouses and partners who are impacted, it's our children, our friends, our bosses, our coworkers, and our clients too. And paired with full-time or part-time work, it can feel like being stretched in too many directions.

Recently, a woman I know told me that the year her mother got sick and passed away, she "pretty much left (her) family" so she could care for her mother. She said her husband was supportive, but he was tired from working every day then driving his busy kids to all of their activities, so he fed the family lots of fast food and takeout. One of the kids gained a noticeable amount of weight. "Their grades suffered too," the mother told me. "I wish someone at their school would have noticed and reached out."

I remember feeling so sorry for myself during the third and final month of my mother's hospice stay. I slept in her room for days at a time, and I missed my kids so much. When I was with my mother, I wanted to be with my kids. When I was with my kids, I wanted to be with my mother. And work may have been at the bottom of the list, but I had promised my boss I could handle my job while my mother was dying, so I turned a small room under the main staircase of the hospice home into my temporary office. I used it to take calls or when I needed to focus on a writing assignment. If anything happened to my mother while I was working, I would just have to run up one flight of stairs to be at her side.

One day I overheard another visitor supervising her children's homework over the phone. She and I had always smiled at one another when we saw each other in the family kitchen, but I had never had the energy to strike up a conversation with her before. "Sounds like our kids are the same age," I finally said to her.

"Mine are in Florida," she told me. "This is my second extended trip here and I am trying to parent them, but it is so hard."

My heart broke for her. I at least lived in the neighboring town and could go home to see my kids at any time if I really wanted or needed to. And I could work from pretty much anywhere. Who knows if she had to leave a job, a career, for this second extended trip.

TRAINING FOR A MARATHON

My situation and the situations of those two mothers were what I call contained pain: difficult, but with an end in sight. While none of us knew exactly when our caregiving roles would stop, we knew our mothers' deaths were imminent. It wasn't easy leaving our children temporarily, but we knew it was just that—temporary. Perhaps more difficult, at least in a different way, are the caregiving situations that have no anticipated ending, the ones that maybe are less dramatic but equally draining. When you have a timeline and can anticipate the ending, it is easier to make choices. "My mother has months to live. I will visit her three times per week." Or, "My father is in the hospital, I will leave work early and visit him until he is discharged." We explain to our partners, our children, our friends, and our bosses that there is a family crisis and we need to focus on it. We bargain with ourselves too: we tell ourselves we can put our lives on hold, just until this is over, and that's okay; I'm where I need to be. The expectation all around is that the situation is short term. And so we make sacrifices, as do the people who depend on us. Often we replace a specific activity with our caregiving duties. We have our partner or neighbor drive the kids to school and activities, for example, or we have a coworker pick up the slack at work. We skimp on sleep or skip the gym. But according to data from the National Alliance for Caregiving and AARP, the average time someone cares for an aging family member is four years, and 15 percent of all unpaid caregivers provide care for ten years or more.[2] So when caregiving isn't a sprint but rather a marathon, how do we determine whose needs come first and therefore how we spend our time?

Women especially can struggle with balancing eldercare and their other roles in life for a number of reasons. For starters, we're tired. The Centers for Disease Control and Prevention report that women are more likely than men to often feel very tired or exhausted.[3] It's no wonder. Most women I meet are busy and overscheduled, juggling many competing priorities and relationships—spouses, children, parents, coworkers, friends. If we are mothers, we are likely doing twice the amount of housework and childcare our spouses do.[4] We are more likely to be the person taking care of pets[5] and we are 30 percent more likely than men to volunteer.[6] The stress of managing it all can feel unbearable.

Consider how a typical woman might spend her time each day, according to data from the American Time Use Survey.[7] She spends approximately an hour eating, 2.2 hours on household activities, and two hours caring for her kids, if she has any. She gets an average of eight hours of sleep per night, takes roughly one hour to shower and dress, works an average of 8.9 hours, and spends approximately one hour a week commuting to work. Now if she has children and adds eldercare to her list of responsibilities, she'll spend 2.3 hours per day caring for her parent or parents. And if she doesn't have children? She'll spend 3.4 hours caring for her aging relative. If you do the math, you see both scenarios add up to more than 24 hours. And that doesn't include the invisible tasks, which aren't accounted for in any time use surveys. Invisible tasks are the things that if we do, no one notices, but if we don't, things start to fall apart. They are tasks like filling out school forms, calling the insurance company to handle a claim, or checking to see if the doctor wrote the prescription with refills. They are things like making sure your child never runs out of Pampers and your parent never runs out of Depends. These tasks take mental energy and time too. But we can't add more hours to the day; the Egyptians and their sundials pretty much set the schedule many years ago and it won't be changing any time soon. So when we add eldercare to an already packed life, what gives?

TIME MANAGEMENT IS NOT THE ANSWER

Basic arithmetic tells us we cannot fit twenty-eight, or even twenty-five, hours in a twenty-four-hour time slot. I've tried. I remember one day, several years before my parents hit crisis level, back when I was merely helping them with some household chores and accompanying them to doctor's visits, that I could have used a few extra hours.

My mother asked me to drive her to a doctor's appointment on Cape Cod, so I took a vacation day. I was lucky to be able to do that. The United States is one of thirteen countries in the world that does not guarantee paid time off[8] and many workers are not covered by the Family Medical Leave Act (FMLA), which means if they take a day off to help an aging parent, they lose a day's pay. (I'll talk more about FMLA and how to access time off in chapter 4.)

I knew from experience that these trips always took longer than planned. Still, I was overambitious in scheduling my day. An editor at *The Huffington Post* had asked me to write an essay, due that day, and of course I hadn't started it. And I had a speaking engagement in Boston that night. How would I fit it all in? Even with a flexible job like mine, my multiple priorities were taking a toll.

I woke up at 5:30 that morning so that I could send some emails to clients and coworkers to keep some projects moving while I was out of the office. Then I saw the kids off to school, showered, and was in my car headed to my mother's house by 9 o'clock. On the way, I dictated my article into my iPhone. How fitting that the topic was my perspective on the highly discussed article by Anne-Marie Slaughter in *The Atlantic*, "Why Women Still Can't Have It All."

I arrived at my mother's house at 10:15 with just enough time to get her in the car and take her across town to her appointment. But when I walked in the house, I heard the shower running; my mother was just stepping into it.

"Mum, what are you doing? We have to go!"

"Liz, please," she said. "Don't start on me. I just couldn't rush this morning."

Oh, *you* couldn't rush.

Amazingly, the doctor had a later opening, but now my whole day was pushed back. After the appointment, a routine checkup, all I wanted to do was go home and work on my never-ending to-do list, but I couldn't just leave. I'd feel too guilty. So I took my mother to lunch and then to the pharmacy for some new prescriptions. When we got back to the house, my father asked me to help him with his computer—he was having trouble logging on. I left their house at 3 o'clock, stressed that I had stayed so long.

As I was driving home, I heard a strange noise coming from under the car. I tried to ignore it for about a mile, but it was persistent. I pulled onto the shoulder of the highway, got out, and lay down to see what was causing the noise. A very large branch was lodged up into the bottom of the car. As I was on my back tugging at it and trying to dislodge it, I had a huge fight with my husband—in my head—about how I should have seen the branch and been more careful not to run over it (him), and how he should be concerned that I didn't get run over on the side of the road instead of worried about the car (me).

I got home just before 5 o'clock, spellchecked and emailed my story, brushed my teeth, put on a dress and lipstick, and left for my speaking gig. One day, I hoped, I would be the kind of keynote speaker who shows up with a blowout and perfect makeup. But that night I was grateful my teeth and dress were clean as I stood up in front of a group of new mothers and gave them tips for balancing career and life so they could be just like me. Oh, the irony! As I drove home, close to midnight, I thought to myself, perhaps out loud, "Enough about working mothers. What about the working daughters?"

As someone who authored a book on working motherhood, I was aware that there are volumes of articles and books for mothers about how to manage career and children, and an endless number of support systems in place. New mothers have baby showers where friends and family celebrate their changing lifestyle and give them practical gifts. They have Mommy & Me classes, Mom's Night Out, and mother's groups at work, where they can swap stories and advice. But if you are a working daughter, too often you are going it alone in figuring out how to balance your career and your aging parents' needs, let alone the needs of your children and spouse. And friends rarely offer you advice—solicited or not. Instead too many working daughters tell me their friends disappear, frustrated by a caregiver's inability to make or keep plans.

When I first started looking for advice, usually around 3 a.m., the time my stress-induced insomnia would kick in, I couldn't find anything useful. I would enter phrases like "balancing elderly parents and marriage" or "balancing elderly parents and work" into Google, but my search results weren't very helpful. I'd either find government websites with hyperlinks to nowhere, or blogs, often hosted by home health agencies, that offered useless platitudes about caregiving as a blessing and useless advice like just talk openly with your family and your boss. If only it were that simple. Not only did these sites not help, they actually hurt. Tired and desperate in the middle of the night, reading them made me feel like I must be the only one struggling to manage it all.

Maybe I couldn't find any useful tips on how to handle my overbooked schedule or complete all of my caregiving tasks because, as I eventually came to learn, managing eldercare is not about the hours in the day or the length of your to-do list. It's about knowing what's important in life. The most grounded and balanced working daughters I know are not slaves to their schedules, but what they are is crystal clear on what matters most to them, and they have set their priorities accordingly.

WHAT MATTERS MOST

Do you know what matters most to you? I suspect that you do, on some level, even if your answer to that question was "no" or "I'm not sure." But to help you get really clear and articulate what exactly does matter to you, you first need to say goodbye to your inner good girl and cure your dutiful daughter disease.

I'm not the only one who suffers from good girl syndrome. Many caregivers, the designated "ones" in their families, do. Think about it: we are raised to be good daughters, good students, good employees, good wives, good mothers, and then good adult daughters. We work hard to be helpful and nice because that's what we come to believe is expected of us. And often it is. It's not easy to shake this syndrome when we've been conditioned to be so good, but if we don't learn to set boundaries, we end up overcommitted, overbooked, and overtired. So what do you do if you can't say no? Stop trying. Say yes instead. That advice may sound counterintuitive, but it isn't, not if you are clear about what matters most to you.

I have a list of things that I say yes to; I call them my nonnegotiables. These are the things in my life that absolutely are not open to debate. The list isn't very long—three to five items max—and it changes depending on what is happening in my life. But spending time with my kids is always on there and so is earning a living. You know what is never on my list? What other people think I should be doing, housework, and trying to be anything that ends in "est." I don't need to be the thinnest, richest, or smartest. Those things really don't matter to me.

Answer these three questions to help create your list of what matters most to you.

1. What is important to you?

Write down everything that is important to you: friends, family, your children, your partner, your parents, your health, your career, fitness, hobbies, interests, crafts, volunteering, causes. Remember how I instructed you to eliminate the word "should" from your vocabulary? Make sure there are no shoulds on your list. When you think you've finished, take a break for at least one hour, then come back and add some more.

2. What is most important now?

Now review your list of what matters and divide it into what is most important at this point in your life and what can wait. What is important but just doesn't need to be a priority for you at this time? Perhaps you want to run a half marathon someday. That's great. But is this really the year, while you're deep into your caregiver role, to fit in long runs?

3. What are your nonnegotiables?

Now look at your list one more time. What three things are most important in your life right now? If you can't choose just three, you can choose five—but no more. This is your list of what matters most. Maybe spending time with a parent is on your list. Maybe volunteering at your child's school made the list. Maybe taking care of your own health or starting a business made the list. Your list won't look like anyone else's. What you end up with are the three to five things you want to say "yes" to every day. Everything else is optional.

SAY YES

When you start saying yes to your nonnegotiable list, saying no to other requests becomes easier. For example, if daily exercise is on your nonnegotiable list, the next time someone asks you to do something that interferes with your workout, say yes to your nonnegotiable and your no becomes clear cut. The more you say yes to what truly matters, the easier it is to find your own version of balance in your life. It may take some practice before it becomes a habit because it's not just our own internal voices pressuring us to be good girls, it's the messages we receive when we watch characters on TV and read magazines, and it's the messages we received from teachers, bosses, and relatives—be agreeable, be accommodating, be a caregiver.

PERFECTION IS OVERRATED

About four years after I ran over that branch while driving my mother home from a doctor's visit, I moved my father from his apartment in an assisted living facility to a shared room in a nursing home. It was a huge change for both of us. My father's dementia had progressed to the point that he no longer knew what year it was, where he was, or sometimes who I was. But I knew. I knew he was my father and that I loved him. I knew that he was now living somewhere he never would have wanted to be. And I knew that I wanted to be with him as much as possible to help him adjust to his new home.

This phase of caregiving was soul crushing, and it was not contained pain. I had no way of knowing how long my father would live. Sure he was ninety, but I had always told him he was too mean to die, and I half believed this to be true. I wanted to spend as much time as I could with him, every day if possible, ideally before he would "sundown," the term used to describe the time of day when a patient's dementia symptoms worsen, which, for him, was usually right after dinner.

Logistically, it was a difficult goal to achieve. My official work hours were Monday through Friday from 8:30 to 5:30, and often later, as most of my coworkers and clients were three hours behind me in California. Weekends were more flexible, but my daughter had soccer games every Saturday and Sunday, usually on fields that were more than an hour away.

My list of nonnegotiables at the time was to be present in my kids' lives, to support my father during this phase of his life, and to stay employed. That was it. I wasn't looking to get ahead in my career. Years of caregiving had made me tired, plus burying one parent and watching another slip away made me want to spend as much time as I could with family. I just didn't have the passion for work I once had.

Being present in my kids' lives meant I tried to make it to every one of my daughter's soccer games on the weekends, and I refused travel when my son had events at school. Staying employed meant I still had to deliver at work and go on the occasional business trip. And supporting my father meant I wanted to visit him daily. Luckily, at that point I was working from home, so on weekdays I snuck away from work to go to the nursing home whenever I could, making sure to check email from my iPhone and not miss any conference calls. If I got behind on assignments, I finished them at night. And on the weekends, I had little time for anything but my dad and soccer. If I had attempted to manage my schedule during that period based on typical time management principles, it never would have worked. I had to focus on what mattered most to me.

I also abandoned all hope of being perfect. Remember, perfect is overrated. And it is an impossible ideal. When you are faced with a daily to-do list three pages long, and when you need to drive your kids to school, create a sales presentation, call the insurance company, fill out a Medicaid application, take your father for an eye exam, and get your daughter to soccer practice by 4:45, perfection just doesn't work. As a working daughter, you need to make some choices. Again, where are you going to crush it and where are you going to cruise?

Most days I was able to visit my father during his good hours before dinner, but sometimes I could only stay for fifteen minutes. Some days I got there after his confusion kicked in or I didn't get there until after his bedtime, so I would sit next to him while he slept. It wasn't perfect, but it was good enough.

Going for good enough may sound easy—after all it's a downgrade from perfection—but it isn't so simple either. It requires you to make a shift and loosen up a little. This isn't easy for caregivers because most of us are desperate for some control. We are powerless over aging and illness, so we often double down trying to maintain order in our lives. But that rarely works. In order to prioritize what truly matters, we need to let go a little. To be good enough you've got to first change your thinking, then change your words, and finally change your behaviors.

The three steps to good enough are as follows.

1. Change your thinking.

A key difference between perfectionism and good enough is how you think about and react to situations. If you think you're the only one who can take your mother to the grocery store, or sort her medication, or clean her house, you are wrong. True: no one else will do these things the same way you do. False: your way is the only or best way.

If your father has a nonurgent but important doctor's appointment and you cannot miss your shift at work or your daughter's dance recital, and you think it will be catastrophic for your Dad to miss his appointment, you are wrong. Ask yourself, what is the worst thing that will happen if I postpone? If the answer isn't Armageddon, then reschedule. A perfect person might think he or she can be in three places at once, but you are simply good enough. You'll take him next week.

If you think you are the only one who can perform your job, you are wrong. Sure, being considered indispensable at work gives you a sense of job security and might score points with the boss, but there are always aspects of your job you can delegate or ask a peer to handle while you are out. Prioritize the tasks you are uniquely qualified to do and offload the rest when caregiving pulls you away from work.

If you are stressed about the fact you haven't been home for dinner in three days because your parent is in the ICU, ask yourself: Will this matter in five years? The answer is no. What will matter is that you were with a family member when he or she was vulnerable and needed an advocate. In five years your kids won't remember those three dinners. They will remember you were a loving and caring daughter who set a great example for them. They will remember the aggregate, and your mothering is bigger than any one night at the dinner table.

2. Change your words.

Erase three words from your vocabulary: "should," for the reasons we already discussed, plus "always" and "never." Remember there are no shoulds. Always and never also have no place in the world of good enough. If you catch yourself using the words always and never—"I will never get it all done," or maybe, "I am always the one who has to . . ."—you are thinking like a perfectionist. When you are good enough, you know that if something doesn't go your way, maybe it will the next time.

3. Change your behaviors.

If you really want to be good enough, you need to practice by changing some of your behaviors. This might be the most challenging part. Here are some suggestions for you try:

- Leave dirty dishes in the sink overnight. Don't make your bed. Stop straightening or curling your hair. It may sound silly, but try making small changes and get used to how it feels.
- Order your parents' groceries online instead of going to the store even if you can't get the exact brand of detergent or butter they like. Use that time to call a friend or take a nap. The world won't come to an end.
- Stop playing the role of office wife. You don't need to be the one to bring in birthday cakes for your coworkers or decorate the office for Halloween. First of all, no one needs more snacks at work, and second, someone else will probably step up and plan the office parties.
- If you can only fit in exercise once a week, or for only ten minutes a day, do it. Forget about that perfect workout. Something is better than nothing. It may not blast fat, but it will have a positive effect on your overall well-being.

By practicing letting go and lowering your expectations, you'll build your adaptability muscles. Give it a try. Go for good enough. It gets easier with practice and it's an effective strategy for managing caregiver stress.

And remember to let the important people in your life know your plan. When my father moved to the nursing home, I shared my feelings with my husband—without using any four-letter words. I told him how much my father's decline and move was tearing me up inside. I told him that I wanted to be with my father every day. And I asked him to accept that I was going to let a lot of other things slide. He in turn told me how he felt when it seemed like I went running whenever my parents needed me. But he also told me he knew how much my father meant to me and that he understood what I needed to do. This time around I felt supported.

I let my boss know that my father's dementia was progressing and she in turn let my peers know that I was going through a tough time. I wasn't the only one with personal challenges, so we started doing a "temperature check" at the beginning of our management team meetings to get a sense of who might need some leeway each week and who might be able to provide assistance.

I talked to my kids too. They knew my father's recent hospitalizations and advancing dementia had rendered me sad and stressed, and they knew I wanted to take care of him as best as I could. And once again I relied on Peg the hospice nurse's words to get me through. I wasn't going to be home much for the unforeseeable future, but hopefully I was setting an example for my children of what unconditional love looks like.

Chapter Four

Flex

"Your mother should come live with you," my mother's primary care physician declared, in front of my mother. "Why isn't she getting out more? You don't call her every day?"

I felt like I was shrinking in his cold, sterile exam room. "I travel a lot," I remember saying, or maybe I stammered. "My sister calls her every day."

I don't know how to do this, I thought to myself. My parents need more than I can give them. I wondered if maybe I shouldn't work so much, if I should go part time. Maybe we could get by on less money? Maybe it was selfish of me to spend time promoting my recently published book instead of spending more time with my parents? I even thought about being less present as a parent. My kids would be fine without me, wouldn't they? They had their father, and I could always spend more time with them when my parents were gone.

The doctor swiveled on his stool and proceeded to tell me about a seminar he had attended, at Harvard he noted, about the importance of socialization for the elderly. My chest tightened. I wanted to scream, "If you cared so much about the elderly, you'd stop lecturing me and find a way to help me help her," and "Can't those Harvard brains find a way to make this easier?" But I didn't want to upset my mother, who really liked this doctor, so I just sat there while he shamed me.

"What do you do for work? How much do you travel? Why do you work so much? What about your husband? How many kids do you have?" I was waiting for, "Why do you work?" but he stopped short of asking that. At some point he mentioned that his mother lived in Pakistan. I guess she was someone else's responsibility; perhaps his sister's?

"I need to work!" I thought to myself "I'm the breadwinner in my family! I have two kids who want to see more of me! You know nothing about my life and I am doing the best I can!"

But I felt defeated. The weight of all that I should have been doing for my parents and all that I was already doing in my day-to-day life was crushing me.

I was aware of the research that said half of all mothers thought they'd be happier if they didn't work.[1] Personally, I never wanted to give up my job because of my children. There were challenging days—when, as babies, they kept me up all night, or when they were sick or had days off from school and I had no childcare, or when I had to travel and I knew they wanted me at home. But for the most part, white collar, suburban working motherhood was somewhat predictable and fairly manageable. All I had to do was pay careful attention to the school calendar so I could schedule days off to attend events and get to know the mothers who could drive to soccer practices and karate lessons that started at 4:00 in the afternoon, because my train didn't get me home from work until 6:40. But working daughterhood, that's a different challenge altogether.

"I thought returning from maternity leave was hard," said a woman who was caring for her mother with metastatic lung cancer and working as a creative director at a digital agency. "I am much more apt to roll into work these days with a pony tail, no makeup, a wrinkled outfit, and a blank look on my face than I was in those days,"

I was too and I discovered that balancing eldercare, plus a career, plus parenting, required the flexibility of a yogini.

KEEP YOUR HOUSE IN ORDER

The parable about the frog and the boiling water often comes to mind when I think about eldercare. According to this story, a frog will immediately jump out of boiling water but a frog in tepid water that is brought to a boil slowly won't perceive the impending danger and will be cooked to death. Caregivers can easily suffer a similar fate. For many women, caregiving starts with little things—helping with bills or household chores. Then you might begin to run errands and chauffeur your parents to doctor's appointments. Before you realize it, you've added a significant number of tasks and wonder why you are all of sudden feeling so overwhelmed. Because you don't notice the increase in responsibilities as they occur, you don't necessarily make the adjustments necessary to accommodate caregiving in your already busy life.

Or the crisis call comes when you're at work, or sound asleep in the middle of the night, or at your child's soccer game, like it happened to me. Something's wrong. Someone fell. An ambulance was called. And without any warning, you're at DEFCON 2. And when that call comes, you better hope you've got your proverbial house in order.

Both times I was preparing for maternity leave, I got really organized at work. I cleaned out my email inbox. I made sure all of my important documents were saved on the company server, not just on my hard drive, so that any of my coworkers could find and access them. And most importantly, I kept a list of all my clients' contact information, the projects I was working on, the status of each project, and any items that needed to be handled while I was out on leave. I updated that list at the end of every day throughout the last month of my pregnancy, saved the updated version to the server, and left a printout on my desk. In case my babies came early, I wanted to be prepared, and I wanted my coworkers to be able to step in and cover for me without too much hassle.

But when my parents got sick and I took off from work to care for them, I was completely unprepared. Unlike with my children, when I knew, give or take a few weeks, when I was going to leave work, my eldercare crisis struck without warning. When I left for my parents' house that Sunday afternoon following the alarming call from my sister, I didn't plan to be gone from my home and my work for a full week.

I've always been terrible about submitting expense reports at work. And while having a corporate credit card makes the process easier, I am still always late turning in my receipts. The week I was on Cape Cod, admitting my father to the ER and my mother to respite care, I got an email from the office manager: *Your receipts were due last week. If you don't get them to me by tomorrow, I will have to tell [our boss].* Damn!

I couldn't fault the office manager; she was just doing her job and I was lucky she hadn't reported me sooner. Plus, I hadn't told any of my California coworkers what was going on in my personal life yet, mainly because I hadn't had time. As far as they knew I was at my desk, business as usual. I had to get those receipts to her—but they were scattered around my home office more than an hour away. So on Tuesday night of that stressful week, I left my parents and drove almost three hours round trip to prepare my expense report. My husband was clearly annoyed that I had come home—not to see him or the kids and not to stay. He barely spoke to me except to say, "Gas isn't cheap." The next day I found a local business that had a shipping service and I mailed the receipts Priority Overnight.

That was a valuable lesson: if you have aging parents, you should try to stay as organized at work as you would if you were expecting a baby because there will be a time when you need to drop everything and run out the door. This is not the time in your life to fall behind on assignments. Copy team members on important correspondence. File important documents on the company server and definitely submit your expense reports on time.

Unlike expectant parents, who are usually congratulated and supported by their coworkers when they leave to care for their baby, a working daughter's family commitments are typically unknown to coworkers, who start to wonder why you are out of work, again, or why you are taking yet another personal call in the office. When your eldercare responsibilities do start to interfere with your job, or if you suspect that they might begin to, consider letting your manager know. If you are transparent and you are organized and prepared for an emergency, your coworkers will be better able, and most likely more willing, to fill in for you.

THE TRUTH SHALL SET YOU FREE

It's not always prudent to disclose details about your personal life at work. Think about how secure you feel in your job and what you may know about your manager's attitudes toward work life issues. Perhaps he or she preaches and practices "family first," or maybe you've overheard him or her make disparaging comments about a coworker who took time off for personal reasons. In some instances, sharing the fact that you have challenges outside of the office may cause managers to view you as a weak link, start monitoring your work to look for evidence that your personal life is impacting your performance, or withhold assignments and promotions. You will need to use your best judgment about whether or not to share.

When my parents first got sick, I hesitated to tell my boss because I knew she encouraged employees to take time off when they had to deal with something personal. While her attitude was admirable, I knew it wasn't the right option for me. I needed my paycheck. However, because my situation was clearly impacting my ability to work, I had to discuss it with her.

Ideally, you will feel comfortable talking to your boss or human resources director about your situation. After all, they can't help you balance work and life if they don't know you need help. Plus, you never want to surprise a supervisor. Giving him or her advance warning lets him or her prepare for when the time comes that you do need to take a day off or leave work with no notice.

If you choose to disclose your situation, stick to the basic facts. Do tell your manager that your elderly mother has been hospitalized and that you may need to attend meetings with her medical team or that you are not expecting her to make it. Don't share details about her diagnosis or the fact that you are worried about paying her medical bills. Do share that your elderly father has moved in with you and that you are finding it difficult to get to work on time as you need to assist him in the morning. Don't rant about how your siblings don't help or how difficult it is to put a pair of compressions stockings on him.

Do have some recommendations on how best to cover your work in the event you cannot do it. And be prepared to ask for any support you think you will need. When my mother went to the hospice home and I worked part time, I would often end my day before my coworkers in California even began theirs. Because we communicated primarily over email, we had a few miscommunications that resulted in our missing client deadlines. So I asked my boss if she would appoint one person in the San Francisco office as my contact. I would call him every day before I left for the day and tell him what I needed, and he would make sure the team delivered it to me before they left for the day.

Likewise, be prepared to turn down suggestions that you don't think will be helpful. Your boss may assume you don't want to participate in a meeting or go on a business trip because you have responsibilities at home. But you might actually be thrilled to travel and spend a night in a hotel with turn down service and no one to take care of.

In discussing your eldercare responsibilities at work, you just might discover that others are in similar situations, and together you may be able to influence how your company supports family caregivers and pave an easier path for future working daughters and sons.

THIS IS IMPORTANT

The United States has a long way to go in terms of helping workers manage work and home life. It's no wonder that female employment has been on the decline here for the past decade.[2] And while the challenges of working motherhood are an oft-cited contributing factor,[3] we must recognize and acknowledge the impact of daughterhood too so that we can begin to make career and eldercare more compatible.

One night while riding the commuter train, I overheard a man talking to his wife on his cell phone. "Listen. Take your mother to her doctor's appointment. This is important. If your boss seriously fires you for going, we will deal with it." What an impossible dilemma and brutal reality—having to choose work or family.

As challenging as I found it at times to stretch my vacation and sick days across all of my parents' doctor's appointments, my children's pediatric well checks, school concerts, and parent/teacher meetings, some women don't even have that option. One-third of employees working in the private sector in this country don't receive any paid sick leave benefits.[4] That is untenable.

In addition to paid leave, there are a number of supportive and flexible practices and policies that companies can offer—and working daughters can ask for. Telecommuting, for example, has been proven to boost productivity by as much as 13 percent,[5] plus it allows caregivers to be on site with the person they are caring for, eliminate their commute time, and, quite frankly, skip a shower on days when they just have too much to do. Of course, many jobs require that work is done at a specific location, but more and more jobs can be done anywhere, at least part of the time. I know teachers who work from home on days they're not in the classroom, grading papers or developing curriculum, and radiologists who review x-rays and scans remotely. With some creativity and knowledge, you may be able to arrange your work to better accommodate your life.

But if working from home, the hospice, or the hospital isn't a viable option, there are still ways to ease the pressures of caring while working. Flexible schedules, whether that means allowing employees to choose their own start and end times, work four ten-hour days, or swap shifts, not only give caregivers time to go to doctor's appointments or pick up and drop off at an adult day care program but can positively impact a company's bottom line. A 2016 study by telecommunications company Vodafone reported that 61 percent of companies surveyed said their profits increased when they introduced flexible working policies.[6] But before you ask for these or any other flexible benefits, get prepared.

Here are three things to do before you ask for flexibility.

Read the employee handbook.

Do your homework before you make the request. Understand if what you are asking for is already available, requires a modification to an existing policy, or is completely counter to your workplace culture and policies. Your company's handbook may outline the requirements for working from home or creating an alternative schedule. Think through how you can adhere to those requirements, or not, and mention that when you make your request. Your manager should appreciate that you considered the existing policies when formulating your request.

Follow the leader.

It's always helpful to note what benefits the management team does or doesn't use in order to get a feel for your company's norms. But they're not your only barometer. Also notice what flexible options your peers are taking advantage of. Sometimes the people who shape the work culture the most are the ones who've been around for a long time, are well liked by their coworkers, or aren't afraid to ask for what they want. Do they arrive early or late to accommodate bus schedules, go to the gym at lunch, or telecommute? Think about how your request will fit in with their work styles and consider how you will make your flexibility work for them, not just for you. It's important to understand the unwritten rules as well as the official policies.

Get clear on what you need.

This may sound like an obvious step, but I'm not talking about making a specific request. You're more likely to succeed if you are clear about what you need to make work and life fit, but you're not wedded to one solution. So while your request might be, "Can I work from home three days a week?" what you need is some extra time on those days because those are the days you bring your mother to physical therapy. Knowing that will allow you to negotiate if the boss says no to your request. Maybe you can come in late five days instead of working at home for three. Be flexible to get flexibility.

TRUST IS YOUR MOST IMPORTANT CURRENCY

Of course, the most important way to secure and hold onto work arrangements that allow you to better manage your life is to build and maintain trust at work. Trust is the currency you trade when life gets messy and performing at work gets challenging.

Here are three steps to build that trust so that you can access the flexibility your life requires.

If you're at work, work.

If you opt to go to work, then you need to do just that. I used to manage a guy who would tell me, "Liz, I'm not 100 percent today, so I won't be doing much." What?! I would have been open to, "I'm not 100 percent today so can we push that deadline, or get an extra set of eyes on that, or can I work on an easier task today?" But "Hey, I'm here but you can't count on me to do jack" didn't really fly. If you show up for work, the expectation is you can work. If you know that you'll need to take calls from home, a doctor, or an insurance rep, tell people up front that you may need to step out of the office for a few minutes or that you will be checking your phone during a meeting. But if you plan to play Candy Crush or look at Facebook all day, call in sick.

If you work from home, work.

Sometimes I see emails from coworkers that say, "I am working from home today. I will reschedule all of my calls." Why? Working from home implies you will be at home, doing work. To make that happen, you may need to set boundaries with your parents, neighbors, kids, and friends. It's perfectly okay to tell them that you are unavailable during work hours. If a call from your sister to "talk about Mom" distracts you, tell your sister you can't talk during work hours—except in a crisis. And then define what a crisis is and isn't. Also make sure you have what you need to be productive. If you don't have access to the company server or a reliable Internet connection and doing your job depends on those things, you are not working from home; you are giving flexibility a bad name.

Take time off if you need it.

Sometimes taking a day off or longer is the best way for you to deal with caregiving-related issues. Once again, check the employee handbook to see what options are available to you. The 1993 Family Medical Leave Act (FMLA) may be an option *if* you are eligible for it. Only employers in the private sector with fifty or more employees are covered by FMLA. And only employees who have worked 1,250 hours during the twelve months prior to the start of leave, work at a location where the employer has fifty or more employees within seventy-five miles, and have been at the company for at least twelve months are eligible. If you and your employer meet the criteria, FMLA allows you to take unpaid leave for specified family and medical reasons such as caring for a spouse, child, or parent who has a serious health condition. While on leave, your job is protected and you can continue your group health insurance coverage under the same terms and conditions as if you had not taken leave. Employees can take up to twelve work weeks of leave in one year and twenty-six weeks if they are caring for a military service member. Note: This is a broad overview of a complex benefit. Make sure to consult with the U.S. Department of Labor website for the exact coverage and eligibility requirements.

KEEP CALM AND CARRY A HAT

As an experienced caregiver, I knew that whenever I took my father to the doctor, I should always plan for it to take twice as long as I thought it would. So one October day, when I took him to get a simple blood pressure check, I planned to be away from my home office for an hour, hour and a half max. Rookie mistake.

On the way to the appointment, my father told me he'd been having some stomach problems. I told the nurse, and she gave him a thorough exam while I averted my eyes and thoroughly examined my email on my iPhone. Some medical professionals want family members to stay in the exam room when their parents undress in case they need help. Eventually, you do get used to seeing your father in his boxers.

"Do you suspect C. diff?" I asked.

C. diff is a bacterial infection that causes diarrhea and is very hard to cure. I spent my caregiving years in fear of it.

"Yes," she said. "Your father needs to follow a BRAT diet, bland foods like bananas, rice, applesauce, and toast."

"YOU CAN'T HAVE ANY ALCOHOL OR DAIRY SIR," she told my father very loudly, as if he were deaf, and she spoke in a singsong voice as if she was talking to a baby. She also informed him that he would need a new prescription to treat this infection.

Then she turned back to me with a series of instructions: "Bring this paperwork to checkout, go downstairs to the lab to get your father a blood test, and bring a stool sample back this afternoon."

I was typing notes into my phone as she spoke. No cheeseburgers or ice cream. Go to lab. Bring a stoo . . . what?!?

"How do I even do that?" I asked. "I don't know how to do that."

She told me the lab could help me. So my father and I went to the lab, where the technician drew blood and then handed my father two collection cups and pointed to the fill line. My father was nodding but he wouldn't be the one collecting the specimen.

"You need to explain that to me," I said. Separate liquids and solids? Freeze one of the samples? What?!?

"How am I supposed to do this?"

"I might have a hat," he answered and stepped away.

Did he just mention a hat? I pictured a baseball cap. I was confused. He came back and handed me a hat. It was a plastic container that I could place in the toilet and collect whatever went in the bowl. He looked like he had solved my problem.

"Yeah, but how am I supposed to do this?"

Now he was the one who was confused.

"I have a client call in five minutes. I have to answer an email, and I'm supposed to be at work today. Something about a freezer??? And . . . how?"

"I can't answer your work questions ma'am." He exhibited zero compassion for the distraught, middle-aged woman in front of him.

"Screw you," I thought to myself.

"Let's go Dad." I was grateful for the oversized Jackie O style sunglasses I was wearing because now I was fighting back tears. I can handle a lot, but I did not think I could handle that.

I took my father back to assisted living, told him to go have a dairy-free lunch, stopped by the nurse's office to ask for help—she gave me a pair of latex gloves—and drove home to get my laptop.

I was so anxious about the collection process, I knew I would not be able to focus on anything else. So when I finally got back to my father's, I sent an email to my coworkers notifying them that I was taking the day off due to a family situation. Then I placed the hat in the toilet and went to the dining room to find my father.

And then, we waited. All day. Emails came in from my coworkers.

"Thinking of you Liz."

"Family comes first Liz."

"Please let us know what we can do." If only.

At 4 p.m. I stepped out into the hall to call the doctor's office. The nurse practitioner was with a patient so the receptionist offered to take a message.

"I've been here all day. I have nothing. I was supposed to be at work. You didn't even give me gloves. I had half a bagel at 7:30 this morning. I haven't eaten since. I'm hungry and tired and I'm going to have to work all weekend to make up for today. My daughter doesn't have a Halloween costume yet. What's the plan?"

"I'm not sure what message you want me to leave," the receptionist replied.

"Tell the nurse that this is not my full-time gig. The day is almost over and I need to know what plan B is."

I went back into the apartment to discover I had what I needed.

On the way back to the lab, I checked my voicemail. The nurse practitioner must have called while I was cleaning out the hat. Her singsong voice was back. "Liz, if you can't get a sample today, just go back and try tomorrow. Have a great night."

I finally returned home at 5:30.

"How was your day?" my husband asked.

"Shitty."

A PERFECT STORM

And then there were times I thought I'd be productive at work but was wrong.

One winter, my mother fell and broke her wrist. I worked with the discharge coordinator at the hospital to place her in a rehab facility while she received physical therapy. She didn't like the facility, so some nights I would drive three hours round trip after work to visit her and try to cheer her up. Despite her unhappiness, I was glad to have her out of her house because it was a very snowy winter and I would worry if she was at home when it stormed.

When meteorologists warned that a massive blizzard was on the way, I offered to bring my father to my house for the night, even though I knew he would refuse.

"Fine, stay there," I told him when he turned me down, "but I have two requests. If you lose power, check in with me via your cell phone and don't go outside until someone shovels you out."

The storm started after midnight and by the time I woke up the next morning, my father's house had no electricity or phone. He wasn't answering his cell. At 11 a.m. his neighbor called me. I had hired her son to shovel, plow, and check on my father.

"I am so relieved to hear from you," I said. "Is my father okay?"

"We don't know," she said. She told me the snow was too deep for her son to cross the street and that maybe after he had some hot cocoa he would try. This was her *adult* son we were talking about.

"Thanks for nothing," I thought.

At noon, I called the police and asked if they would check on my father. By 3 o'clock that afternoon, I still hadn't heard from them, nor had I done any work. . . I couldn't concentrate. I was too worried, so I called again.

"Oh, we sent an officer out to your father's house and he wasn't home," they told me.

"That's impossible," I said.

"He must have gone to the shelter at the high school," the officer said.

"He didn't." My father would never do that. "You need to go back. My father is hard of hearing and may be sleeping. Please go around to the back of the house and bang on his bedroom window."

At 4 p.m., my phone rang.

"Ma'am. This is the police dispatcher. One of my officers found your father at home. He is in the backyard chopping wood for his stove."

"Is your officer still there?" I asked.

"Yes, ma'am."

"Tell him to shoot to kill."

I was furious. I had to write a newsletter for one client and a press release for another and they were both due the next day. But I had spent the whole day worrying and had gotten nothing done. It was going to be a long night.

Fortunately, or unfortunately, my coworkers got used to my being distracted. A few years later, I was in a company meeting in San Francisco when my phone rang. I recognized the number—my father's nursing home—and so I jumped out of my seat and answered the phone before I had even walked out of the conference room, my pulse quickening as it always did when someone called me from there.

It was one of the nurses. "Hi Liz. I'm not sure what time you're coming by today . . ."

"I'm not! I'm in California! What's wrong?!"

"Nothing is wrong. Your father has a rather large blister on his right heel. I just wanted you to know we are aware of it and treating it."

I walked back into the conference room as my colleagues were considering ways to handle a challenging client. I burst out laughing; I couldn't help myself. They looked up.

"My Dad has a blister!" I exclaimed.

Whether I was sidelined by stools or snowstorms or simple phone calls from the nursing home, I always tried to honor my deadlines. That's because I knew that being able to blend care and career is a luxury, one that too few women are able to benefit from. If you do have flexibility at work, keep in mind that it is a privilege, not a right.

In order to maintain that privilege, follow these five guidelines.

Underpromise, and then deliver.

As a working daughter, a caregiver, you are probably prone to people pleasing. Be careful! Don't take on more than you can handle. Don't load up your proverbial plate at work with more responsibility, projects, and aggressive deadlines than you can actually digest. When it comes to flexing to accommodate eldercare, underpromise and then, if you can, overdeliver. Tell your boss you can have a report to them by Wednesday, even though you know you can complete it, and deliver it, by Tuesday. What you never want to do is promise that report on Wednesday but not be able to complete it until Thursday. By underpromising and overdelivering, you won't leave anyone at work in a lurch and you actually have the breathing space to focus on whatever you need to in your personal life.

Remember it's on you to make flex work.

When my mother began hospice care, and I reduced my work hours by 50 percent, my schedule allowed me the time to focus on my family, but it actually made getting my work done challenging. I mentioned there were a few miscommunications with my colleagues in California. One day I asked them to finish a presentation—they just needed to select photos for a few slides. I told them I would not be on email for the rest of the day so to go ahead and send the presentation to our client without my reviewing the photos they chose. Later that night, after my mother had fallen asleep, I looked at my email. Not only had one of my team members asked for my input on the photos she selected, she wrote that she wouldn't send the presentation to the client until I weighed in. I was annoyed with her and stressed that the assignment wouldn't get to the client on time. I wanted to fire off a scathing email about her inability to follow instructions, but instead I finished the presentation and sent it myself. Ultimately, making my flexible schedule work was my responsibility. Sometimes flex is messy and sometimes your coworkers let you down. Deal with it and move on.

Doctors aren't corporate, but you can still try.

Just like it's not up to your coworkers to make your flex work for you, it's not up to the doctor's office either. In the corporate world, I'd never call a meeting without confirming that the schedule worked for all participants. In the medical world, it happens daily. You go to the checkout window to book your mother's next appointment and the staffer gives you a date and time that works for the doctor but might be incredibly inconvenient for you. Guess what? You don't have to accept that appointment. You can inquire about openings before work, at the end of the day, or on Tuesdays because you don't have to drive carpool that day. Let your parents' medical team know your schedule limitations and competing priorities and respectfully ask that you work to find mutually convenient meeting times and communication methods. It won't work out every time—inevitably whenever a doctor returns my call I am in a meeting—but more often than not the care team will appreciate knowing how and when to reach you and what level of involvement you prefer.

Your personal life is personal, not company business.

Err on the side of less is more when it comes to sharing the reason for your flex accommodations with anyone outside of your manager and maybe your immediate coworkers. Sure, it's okay to be human and let people know you are taking some personal time or changing your hours for personal reasons, but you don't need to share all of the details. I always encourage the people I manage to adopt a don't ask, don't tell policy. I won't ask you why you need to leave at 2:30 on Wednesday, and please don't tell me. Instead tell me what work I can expect from you, when I can expect it, who I can call in your absence, and when you'll be available again. Those are the details you need to communicate when you make a flex request.

Work where and when you can.

I once conducted a client call from an empty wheelchair outside an emergency room. I ran a webinar from the parking lot of an assisted living facility. I held a remote meeting from an ambulance bay. I accepted a delivery of morphine for my mother's end-of-life care while on a management team call where my coworkers were using words like downfunnel and paradigm shift. Work was the last thing I cared about that day, but I had to get paid. When you're a caregiver, be prepared to work where and when you can, like while you're waiting for a doctor who is running late or for lab results that take hours to come back. Keep your phone charged, your wifi hotspot handy, and a laptop or tablet with you at all times. Don't waste precious minutes because you weren't prepared.

THE COST OF FLEX

As grateful as I was for the flexibility I had, I felt like it came at a cost. I was convinced that most of my coworkers were concerned about my productivity, my commitment, and my reliability. And I wasn't alone. A report from the

AARP Institute for Public Policy revealed that workers with eldercare responsibilities "perceive significantly lower job security than workers with childcare needs."[7]

In an interview with the *New York Times*, Joan C. Williams, founding director of the Center for Work-Life Law at the University of California, Hastings College of the Law, said of flex policies, "Informally everyone knows you are penalized for using them. I invented the term 'flexibility stigma' to describe that phenomenon. Recent studies have found that it is alive and well, and it functions quite differently for women than it does for men."[8]

Perhaps if there were more programs to help family caregivers and more public dialogue about the impact of eldercare on the workforce, working daughters wouldn't feel so vulnerable in their jobs. While more and more companies are starting to offer programs to support workers with parents, not just workers who are parents, historically that hasn't been the case.

In 2016, global services company Deloitte announced it would provide up to sixteen weeks of paid leave to eligible employees "to support a range of life events impacting them and their families."[9] I hoped that this initiative would inspire other companies to follow suit. But two years later, most still haven't stepped up. Among the biggest employers, eldercare benefits are still lacking. Walmart's benefits site, for example, boasts maternal, parental, and adoption support, but no mention of eldercare.[10]

According to a 2018 survey sponsored by insurance company Transamerica, out of 1,802 employers nationwide, only 12 percent offered resources and/or tools to support caregivers.[11] It's time someone published a list of Best Companies for Working Daughters, although I fear that list would be short.

Far more impactful than how caregiving makes us feel at work are the financial ramifications working daughters suffer as a result of family responsibilities—the estimated $324,044 they lose over their lifetime due to caregiving. For the majority of caregivers, women in their late forties, this is the time earning potential starts to wane,[12] and by fifty, their job prospects drop off significantly,[13] so it's not a good time to slow down at work.

And we can't forget the growing ranks of young caregivers either. AARP reports that more than ten million millennials between the ages of twenty and thirty are caring for an aging or ill parent or family member.[14] This is a critical time for women to build their professional reputations and advance their career goals.

If a working daughter, especially an older one, steps out of the workforce for a period of time to care for family, chances are high that she won't be able to step back in. According to a 2015 study from the Federal Reserve Bank of St. Louis, half of women over fifty who are unemployed stay unemployed long term.[15] Contributing to this fact is most likely a potent combination of age and gender discrimination.

From a gender perspective, caregiving has historically been viewed as women's work and is sadly undervalued. Family caregivers in the United States provide an estimated thirty-seven billion hours of "free" care to parents, partners, and other adults—worth an estimated $470 billion,[16] based on estimating the number of caregivers per state and multiplying the estimated number of hours of care they provide by the state's minimum wage. But the work a woman does outside the workforce, unpaid, doesn't count when it comes to evaluating her hireability. It should.

Every now and again I come across an article on a business or lifestyle website in which some executive is sharing her perspective on how motherhood has made her better at her job.[17] She's more efficient. She's a better delegator. She has a greater sense of purpose. Not once have I seen an interview with a caregiver about the career gains she's experienced from eldercare. Working daughters need to start touting their skills and strengths because lack of awareness and understanding often leads managers to develop negative perceptions of them. I was once told during a discussion about my work performance that I was a "misfit toy." Even though I had met or exceeded all of my goals that year, my inability to travel due to my caregiving responsibilities was a strike against me. That kind of feedback is not uncommon for working daughters. One told me that after twenty-eight years on the job, her boss told her that her management skills were deficient.

"At my annual review, I was told that I have not been performing up to expectations," another working daughter shared. "But I refrained from pointing out that the deaths of my mother and mother-in-law last year affected me . . . and that I had had to sell my deceased aunt's house, put together the guardianship report for my cousin to submit to the court, and assist my father-in-law in moving to a senior living community."

Working daughters aren't looking for a free pass, just some support. One computer technician said that when she asked for some flexibility to care for her parent she was told, "We don't pay people to be sick or to have family/personal issues—we pay people to work." But a handful of supervisors did support her and helped her rebound and return "to peak work performance." "I always made up for [the flexibility] work wise when I could," she explained. "I was thankful and highly productive because of it."

The truth is, working daughters can make great employees. They develop and hone a number of important skills from their caregiving experiences that can be real assets at work. Working daughters have a strong work ethic. They essentially work multiple jobs each day: the paid job, plus the unpaid one—eldercare—and parenting too. Working daughters have incredible negotiation skills, problem-solving abilities, and pay close attention to detail. They're not just taking their parents to doctor's appointments; they're administering medications, performing medical tasks, marshaling resources, and managing finances. When a day's to-do list includes tasks as wide ranging as taking your father to the doctor, reviewing his care plan at the assisted living facility, running an errand, filling out paperwork for school, helping your kid study for a geography test, editing a corporate blog post, calling a client to answer a question, and calling the insurance company, *and* you get it all done, it's clear that working daughters know how to prioritize time, energy, and resources. Or as a woman who is frequently called to her mother's nursing home to deal with a health-related crisis and works full time for a government agency put it, "We're so good at our jobs that we can still do them well when we're overwhelmed with grief and exhaustion."

It would behoove smart managers to find ways to support and retain caregivers at work. If the skill set isn't a compelling enough case, basic economics should be. According to a study from Met Life, American companies lose between $17.1 billion and $33.6 billion in lost productivity annually due to caregiving.[18] If American businesses are going to keep working daughters at work, and keep them productive while they are there, we need better eldercare benefits like affordable eldercare options, backup eldercare services so working daughters who can afford to hire help can show up for work when the paid caregivers cancel, referrals to resources and care managers, flexibility, and less dependence on a facetime culture, in which if you're not at the office from 9:00 to 5:00, you're not a valuable part of the team.

KNOW YOUR WORTH

If you're feeling undervalued at work, take a few minutes in the morning to remind yourself of your worth so you can show up for work confident that in spite of your personal responsibilities, you are a valuable member of the team. If you feel confident, you are more likely to perform well. And the last thing you need is to worry about your job, and therefore financial security, when you have so much else to deal with.

Here are four strategies to help you feel confident at work when caregiving has left you feeling anything but.

1. Read your bio (or your resume).

Your professional bios, resumes, and LinkedIn profiles extol your accomplishments and professional achievements. You should look at yours more often. Recently I was asked to update my biography in advance of a speaking engagement. I was working at home with a chipped manicure, my gray roots showing, dressed in my husband's fleece, a pair of leggings, and UGG boots. I hardly looked, or felt, large and in charge. But damn, I looked good on paper, and my confidence was immediately boosted. Next time you feel your confidence lagging, review your resume and own it. Yes, *you* did that!

2. Consult your Gold Star folder.

Gold Star folders are where you keep samples of your best work as well as emails, notes of praise, and any accolades that you've received over the years. Sometimes you just need a reminder that you do good work and that other people recognize that and appreciate it. And sometimes your bosses may need a reminder too. If you don't have a Gold Star folder, you should start one—whether it is print or electronic is up to you. Either way, keep it handy and up to date so you can access it whenever you're feeling down or need to prepare for you next performance review.

3. Play your theme song.

In one episode of *Ally McBeal*, a television show about the professional and personal life of a young lawyer that aired in the late 1990s, Ally's therapist (played by Tracy Ullman) tells Ally (Calista Flockhart) to find a theme song, something she can play in her head to make her feel better. It worked for the fictitious lawyer, who chose "Tell Him" by the Exciters—a song that captured Ally's search for love—and it can work for you.[19] On my way to important meetings, I always listen to Katrina and the Waves's "Walking on Sunshine." I can't help but feel positive when I hear it. Choose a song that makes you involuntarily smile and play it loud when you need a boost.

4. Don your armor.

Taking inspiration from another pop culture reference, remember what the indominable Claire Belcher said in the film *Steel Magnolias*: "Our ability to accessorize is what separates us from the animals." "Dress for success" may sound like a cliché, but it's solid advice. Who would Wonder Woman be, after all, without her cuffs? Next time you need to feel confident at work, dress up. It helps.

I GUESS MY BEST WASN'T GOOD ENOUGH

Finally, know that you can do all of the above and still suffer a reputational hit. Every choice you make has a consequence, and sometimes choosing to prioritize your life outside of work affects your status at work. It is important you understand the possible ramifications of the choices you make and know that you made the best decisions you could at the time.

I knew that when I chose to put family first, there would be consequences. What I didn't know was just how hard it was going to be to deal with those consequences. After my mother passed away, I was sad, but I was also somewhat relieved. No more watching my mother die; no more daily visits to the hospice home. I could focus my energy on caring for just one elderly parent, reconnect with my kids who I had mostly ignored during the last months of my mother's life, and recommit to my work goals that had taken a back seat to life for five months. Even though I knew I was one of the lucky ones, working for a boss who allowed me the flexibility I needed, I still felt like a drag on the business as I had hardly been carrying my weight at the office for months. I wished I could have taken a week after my mother's funeral to rest and process all that had transpired, but because I had used up all of my paid time off to be with my mother, I went back to work two days after we buried her and tried to muster my energy to focus on work again.

I was doing pretty well for the first two weeks—dusting off long-term projects, participating in leadership team meetings, and reconnecting with clients. I even gave up a Sunday afternoon to go to New York and visit with a client at a trade show. I thought she would appreciate my interest and commitment. Instead she greeted me by saying, "We've lost too much momentum because of your mother dying." She fired my firm a week later.

The next week, our company found out we hadn't won a project we had pitched a few weeks before my mother died, one that our team had really wanted. The reason? The prospect said I didn't instill any confidence in him. So to instill some confidence in myself, I reminded myself that I had done my best work, my most important work, outside of the office.

Chapter Five

Choose

"Great news. Your mother can go home today." The social worker's words shocked me.

"Home where?" I asked.

When my mother opted out of treatment for her late stage cancer, there was no reason to keep her in the hospital; I understood that. But her attending doctor had told me she would be transferred to a skilled nursing facility, probably for a week, for physical therapy. I thought I could use that week to figure out a plan for her end of life while also touring memory care facilities for my father.

It was July 2, the day after I found out that my mother had ovarian cancer and my father had early stage Alzheimer's and dementia, that he could not live at home, and that I had a week to find a memory care facility for him to spend the rest of his life in. When I asked the social worker handling his case what would happen if I couldn't find a place I liked in that timeframe, she told me, "Then we will place him somewhere we choose."

So when I went to visit my mother on my lunch hour, I was not expecting to hear that she was being released. And I was definitely not expecting to hear that she was being released to me *that afternoon*. I was due back at work in less than an hour.

"I don't know where to take her," I said to the social worker. "She was staying in respite care on the Cape because my father is in the hospital and she can't be home alone."

"Then take her to your house," she said.

What was I supposed to say? Even though my mother had always told my sisters and me, "I do *not* want to live with any of you when I'm old," and we would joke, "Don't worry you're not invited," I suspected given these circumstances she might have changed her mind. But I couldn't take her. My husband and I had an agreement that we would never take our parents in long term.

We had cohabitated with my parents for two weeks when we bought the house I grew up in from them and the house they were building on Cape Cod wasn't finished. My husband complained every single night: my parents hadn't packed yet and their stuff was everywhere, or my father had washed his favorite nonstick saucepan with an abrasive scrub pad, or my parents watched *Law & Order* reruns at a volume so loud that surely people in Rhode Island could hear the show. I would get upset and ask him to keep it down; I didn't want my parents to hear him. And every single night, he would get out of bed, grab a duffle bag as if to pack, and say he was going to stay with his mother until my parents left. And every single night he got back into bed and went to sleep.

A few years earlier, when we were moving back to Massachusetts after spending a year in Texas, we stayed with his mother for a few weeks. Well, my husband did. I only lasted a week. Every night after dinner I would try to be helpful by clearing the table. And every night my mother-in-law would restack the dishes in the dishwasher because, apparently, I did it incorrectly. I loved my mother-in-law and didn't want that to change, so I retreated to my parents' house until our move-in date.

If my husband and I were sure about anything, it was that our no parents agreement was the right decision for our marriage. But now? I didn't know what to do or say as my mother lay in her hospital bed and she and her social worker looked at me.

I'd have to take her, right? Would it be okay for a few weeks? How would that go over? Not well, but I mean, come on; my husband wasn't heartless, was he? Would this mean he could do the same and his mother might move in some day? Where would my mother sleep? We didn't even have a guest bed. I used the spare bedroom as an office. And what if she tripped? There were toys all over the floor. What relationship should I honor: mother/daughter or husband/wife?

I could feel tears welling in my eyes. I stood there for a few seconds not knowing what to do and finally told my mother, "I'll be right back." I think the social worker thought we were done because she started walking down the hall.

"Can we speak in your office?" I asked her.

"Let's just talk here," she said.

If my husband had been there he would have told me, "Unclench the jaw, Liz." I tend to jut the bottom of my mouth backward when I am trying not to explode, as if to lock my mouth shut. And I was ready to explode. I just assumed that a conversation with a distraught, teary-eyed daughter of a terminal cancer patient would take place in an office, not a hallway.

I don't remember what I said to her that day; I only remember how much contempt I felt toward her. Whatever I said helped though. I was given one more day to make arrangements.

IMPLICIT BIAS IN ACTION

That summer, I would have told you that medical professionals just didn't care at all about family caregivers. They certainly didn't seem to grasp that adult daughters might actually be *working* daughters. I thought they just went about their jobs expecting family members to be available at any time, whether to drive patients to or from appointments, to answer their calls, to meet with them at any time of day, or to care for patients when they were discharged—no matter how complex the follow up care might be, and no matter how demanding their jobs might be. I no longer believe that.

I now believe that yes, while there are still a few arrogant doctors roaming hospital halls, and not all social workers are created equal, it's not a lack of caring that leads a caregiver to feeling ignored, undervalued, or judged, as I did that day in my mother's hospital room. It's the fact that medical professionals are dealing with a number of pressures including more strident productivity goals, new technologies, and more documentation requirements, and that can make them seem rushed, inflexible, and uncaring. That and the fact that they, like everyone else, harbor implicit biases.

An implicit bias is an unconscious belief that a person has about a group of people such as women or a religious group or people of a certain race. As a result of that belief, they attribute particular qualities to the group. Working mothers often experience implicit bias at work. A manager or coworker may explicitly believe that both women and men can be qualified candidates for a job, but they may unconsciously think women should be home raising children. As a result, they might be less inclined to hire or promote women.

Working daughters can experience it too. Perhaps the social worker handling my mother's case was operating with an implicit bias that the middle-class, middle-aged woman standing before her had the time and inclination to care for her mother in her home. In my Gap capris, t-shirt, and probably still wet ponytail, I didn't look the part of a busy senior executive, but I was that *and* a concerned daughter.

Implicit bias was evident at a panel discussion I attended a few years ago. The topic was geriatric care and the panel consisted of a doctor, a nurse, two executives from health insurance companies, and the CEO of a national chain of senior living facilities. The panelists used the word "daughter" seven times. Not once did they say the word "son."

These unspoken beliefs are harmful to women. Amid the societal expectations and cultural norms that we should be nurturing and giving and that caregiving is a blessing we should accept with open heart and arms, we feel guilty and judged when we think differently and when we make choices that seem to buck those beliefs. I felt judged that day in my mother's hospital room. I felt judged by my mother's primary care physician months earlier when he implied it's a woman's role to care for her parents and it's a man's role to work for money.

Another working daughter I know finds her mother's doctor judgmental too. She says he is constantly praising her for moving in with her mother to take care of her. At one visit he told her about another patient of his whose adult children moved him to memory care.

"You know what happens once they go there," he said, "They decline fast."

"The implication being," this woman says, "that I'm such a good daughter I would never do that to my mother. But I'm pretty sure that one day I will need to place my mother in memory care." She knows that eventually she won't be able to manage having her mother at home while she is at work and that her doctor will likely judge her for that choice.

Sometimes even praise can be damning. The month of November has historically been designated as National Family Caregiver's Month, and each year the current president writes a proclamation marking the occasion. I remember reading President Obama's last pronouncement in 2016. He said, "The women and men who put their loved ones before themselves show incredible generosity every day, and we must continue to support them in every task they selflessly carry out."[1] Although grateful for the recognition and support, I cringed when I read it. Sentiments like that unintentionally put pressure on family caregivers because that image of the selfless person, while flattering and in some cases true, is almost impossible to live up to for most people—especially the ones trying to balance caregiving with a job. And when we don't live up to the ideal, we feel like we've failed and that we are letting down the people we care for. It would have been selfless to move my mother in with me, and I worried I was letting her down by not offering, but if I had chosen to do what others thought was right for her, I would have been choosing something that was wrong for me. And the healthiest path caregivers can take is to value their own lives as much as they value the lives of the people they care for—and then brace themselves, because not everybody will approve.

WE DO NOT WAGE WAR

It's easy to doubt your choices, especially when you read headlines like this one from *Forbes*: "New Survey Finds Adult Children Want Their Parents to Age at Home."[2] Well, of course the survey reached those findings; it was conducted by a company that provides in-home care! After twenty-six years in marketing, I can sniff out a smart public relations tactic, and that was a good one. Surveys like that are produced to generate headlines. For working daughters trying to determine the best course of action for their families, those headlines can trigger judgment-filled, guilt-inducing reactions about how they care for their aging parents—from family, neighbors, other working daughters, and most of all themselves. And they resemble the ridiculous headlines that fuel the media-stoked so-called mommy wars.

You'd have to live under a rock not to have heard about, or experienced for yourself, the "mommy wars." Newspapers, magazines, blogs, and morning shows periodically serve up a stream of articles and segments about whether breast or bottle is best, whether women are opting out or leaning in, and whose children are better adjusted: the stay at home or the working mother. And these features spur even more discussion in the comment sections and on social media, every post a seeming attack on the other's parenting choices.

If we're not careful, we could find ourselves in the same position— second guessing our own, and others', decisions. And my fellow working daughters, we did not make it through our twenties, thirties, and into our mid-forties, surviving the mommy wars, only to find ourselves fighting daughter wars as we move into our fifties, sixties, and beyond.

The fact is, there is no one right way to do anything when it comes to caregiving, especially when it comes to balancing care with career. And there are very few guides to follow. Unlike many new mothers, you can't necessarily turn to your own for advice, not only because she may be the person you are caring for but also because there are different expectations and norms for each generation, and these norms are influenced by family, cultural, and socioeconomic factors. Your mother may have taken her parents in; your mother may not have worked outside the home. Your grandmothers may have taken your great grandparents in. They lived in another time and possibly in another country with different customs. More often than not, women find themselves on their own in making important caregiving-related decisions.

I believe women have never been at war with each other as much as we've been targeted by companies that want to sell us products and media that want to generate clicks and views. So when marketers release studies that state things like "baby boomers say caring for elderly in their own homes is better than in an assisted living facility," it's not only not helpful, it can also be detrimental. And when a friend, family member, or doctor imparts an unwelcome and uninformed opinion about what's best for you and your elderly parent, it is *absolutely* not helpful and it can make even the most self-confident woman feel judged.

So how do you choose your caregiving path? Do you help your parents age at home or do you move them in with you? Do you steer them toward assisted living or a nursing home? Do you advocate for aggressive medical intervention or suggest palliative care? Do you charge ahead with your career or work on cruise control for a while? How do you balance what is right for you and your parents with the needs of your children, siblings, relatives, and, of course, employer?

BLENDING COURAGE WITH COMPASSION

Aim to act with equal parts courage and compassion. Just as it takes courage to care for someone at home, it also takes courage to acknowledge when you can't provide the best care at home. Compassion comes into play when you consider your parents' feelings and desires. While many people refer to eldercare as a role reversal, when an adult child starts "parenting" his or her parent, it really isn't; it's a shift. Remember that your parents are adults, with their own opinions, values, and wishes separate from yours. Yes, there are times when their decisions impact, and sometimes complicate, your life, like when a parent gives up driving and won't use the senior center shuttle, leaving him or her with no way to go grocery shopping or get to doctor's appointments. But your parents have the right to choose how they live their lives, and you have the right to choose how you respond.

Of course, if a parent suffers from a cognitive impairment and you have power of attorney or guardianship, then you may need to make decisions on his or her behalf without his or her input. Either way, if you only act with courage, you could leave your parents feeling unheard and alone. If you only act with compassion, you could end up feeling like a victim and acting like a martyr.

Keep in mind you are playing a long game. Often when you are caring for an aging parent, you have to make quick decisions, like I did when my mother was released from the hospital. Strive to make the best choices with the information you have at the time and in the amount of time you have to make them. But also keep in mind that your decisions could have long-term implications for you. It might be possible to move your parents in with you today, but if they eventually need more care, how will you leave them alone to go to work? It may be tempting to quit your job to deal with a crisis, but will you be able to reenter the workforce later, and do you have enough in your retirement account to stop working now?

Finally, get clear about what you want for your parents and separate those thoughts from what your parents want for themselves. Whenever there were snowstorms, I would ask my parents to come stay with me until the storm passed, but they always opted to stay home. They'd assure me that they had plenty of food and that they didn't need any refills for their medications, that they had a wood stove, and they would be fine. I would get frustrated and upset with them. "It's not safe. What if you lose power? I will be worried." There it was: *I* would be worried. Asking them to come stay with me was for my peace of mind, not theirs. Your wants will not always match your parents' wants. So how do you know what they want? Ask them.

THE "CONVERSATION"

One Thanksgiving, years ago, my husband, my parents, and I were sitting around my dining room table after dinner, our dessert plates stained blue from the pie we had just eaten, my father still drinking his black coffee.

"Elizabeth," my mother said, "I want to talk to you about something important."

"Ugh," I thought to myself. "Why can't we just relax?" Thanksgiving is my favorite holiday because when the meal is over, I have three glorious days off from work. I didn't want to think or talk about anything important.

"I want to talk to you about my funeral plans."

At that time, my parents had survived a brain tumor, two heart surgeries, and melanoma and were healthy and complication free. A funeral wasn't imminent. My mother, as I would later come to appreciate, was just very prepared. She told me that night that she had purchased a burial plot at the National Cemetery on Cape Cod.

"I want the service on the Cape, and I don't want people to feel like they have to come, but I think having it down there is the most convenient."

"Convenient? Yeah, right," I said. "The cottage will be full because family will be in town for the funeral, which means Eileen and her family will stay at your house, so Kevin and I will have to get a hotel room. Oh, but wait, people will need rides, so I will have to drive up and back. So convenient."

I was trying to be funny. But I failed.

"Wow, Liz," my husband said. "Give her a break."

"I was just trying to make it easy for all of you," my mother said.

SHUT UP AND LISTEN

Looking back, I can't believe what a dope I was. I know now that a parent who initiates a discussion about their end of life plans, especially one who has already done the planning, is like the Holy Grail for adult children. If your parent comes to you ready to discuss his or her funeral plans, current or future living arrangements, what kind of medical intervention he or she will or won't want in the event of illness or incapacitation, or any other issues pertaining to aging or dying, listen up! It's a gift.

A few years after that awkward conversation, and a few weeks after we figured out where "home" would be when my mother was released from the hospital, she asked me to go to her house on the Cape and find a yellow lined sheet of paper in the top drawer of her dining room hutch. I brought it to her new home—an apartment at the assisted living facility down the road from me. On that piece of paper she had written down exactly what she wanted when she died: the music for the church, the dress and necklace she wanted to wear, and a photograph she wanted buried with her. The only thing up for discussion was whether or not she should wear nylons in the afterlife. I told her that would be hell. But mostly I shut up and listened as she reviewed her wishes with me.

IT'S A PROCESS

Chances are that you won't be as fortunate as I was, and that you will have to initiate "the conversation" with your parents. As prepared as my mother was for her funeral, and as open as she was to talking about it, she and my father always shut down any attempts to discuss their living arrangements as they aged. My sisters and I thought their house had become too much of a burden for them, that they were isolated (they no longer drove and were not close to any shopping or social activities), and we wanted them to consider moving. "We're not going anywhere," my father would say. My mother wouldn't say anything at all.

I looked for advice on the Internet but couldn't find anything helpful. Too many of the articles I read assumed "the conversation" would be rational and reasonable. Not with my family! Not this topic! I threatened to pull my help and support if they didn't move, but we all knew that would never happen. I thought about using guilt to get what I wanted, but that didn't feel right and probably wouldn't have worked anyway. I felt like a failure, believing other adult children were more successful convincing their parents to change their living situations than I was. But I was wrong.

I've met plenty of adult children who tried and failed to get their parents to make a change. I've met even more who have never broached the topic at all because they don't know how to do so. It took a crisis for my parents to move, and I've since learned this is quite common and far from ideal.

Here are seven strategies for broaching uncomfortable conversations with your parents so that hopefully it doesn't take a health crisis to effect necessary change on behalf of your own parents.

Understand it's a process.

"The conversation" is actually a series of conversations. Don't expect to visit your parents one afternoon, or to go home for the holidays, suggest that Mom or Dad or your Great Aunt Gracie can no longer live independently, and get them to say, "You're so right. Let's make a move." Don't try to cram the conversation in when you stop in to visit them on your way home from work. And definitely don't bring up sensitive subjects when you have looming deadlines at the office or a big project due to your boss at the end of the week. Important issues are rarely resolved through one conversation and cannot be rushed.

Flip the dynamic.

Some of us resist future planning with our parents because we think it requires us to bring up potentially difficult or unpleasant conversations. We worry if we bring up their finances, they might think we're angling for inheritance. We don't want to raise the need for an advanced directive, a document outlining medical wishes for intervention, because who wants to talk about illness and dying? We think if we suggest their home is no longer the best place for them, we are forcing them to acknowledge that they are failing.

So rather than raising these issues, ask your parents to share their vision for their future with you. Ask them what matters most to them in the next phase of their life. Is it independence? Leaving money to their grandchildren? The best medical care they can receive? Spending time with family? What are their values at this point in their life? A conversation about what someone wants is much more positive and optimistic than a conversation about what someone may no longer be able to do.

Listen first.

What are you hearing and how can you address it? If your parents want to age at home, what will make that a reality? Will they need help with shopping and driving? Will they need a visiting nurse or home health aide? Or maybe they tell you they don't want to be a burden to their children. Okay, what does that look like for both of you? Would moving them closer to you help? Would hiring a housecleaner help? Are they resistant to those ideas? Then what are some other approaches? And if they shut the conversation down, remember it's a process. Back off and revisit the discussion at a later date.

Go for small wins.

Consider if there are small steps you can take to advance the conversation. Rather than aiming for, "Hey mom, I think it's time for you to move into assisted living," try "Mom, Aunt June just moved into Sunset Studios. I hear it's really nice. Want to stop by, see her, and check it out?" Your mother might agree but add, "Sure but don't think I'm ever going to a place like that." Let it go. Celebrate the small win. She agreed to see the place, didn't she? Every conversation you have on this topic will help you and your parent get more comfortable addressing how to face the next phase of his or her life. Maybe you think your parents should give you power of attorney, authorization to represent them or act on their behalf in financial, medical, and legal issues, but they aren't comfortable with that. Will they at least add you to their bank account so you can help with bill paying if needed, or name you as their healthcare proxy so you can speak with their doctors? Baby steps are still progress.

Get the facts.

If you can enter the conversation with knowledge of your parents' financial information, do it. The more data you have, the better you'll be able to address their fears and concerns. Likewise, if you're talking about a possible move, gather information about what facilities are available, which ones have openings, and how much they cost. Have the facts but present them as options.

Value autonomy as well as safety.

Maybe you think your parent should move or accept in-home assistance because you are concerned about his or her safety. And maybe, like my father who insisted on renewing his license and climbing ladders to clean his gutter in his mid-eighties, your parents value their freedom over their safety. Go ahead and tell them why you are concerned and how their decisions might impact you. "If you fall off the ladder and get hurt, I will have to take time off of work to care for you." But remember you are dealing with an adult and ultimately the decision is his or hers. And if your parent chooses a path that you don't like, ultimately you too have a choice. If my father had fallen off that ladder—if I hadn't stolen it—I wouldn't have *had* to take care of him, but I would have chosen to take care of him. Likewise when my mother was no longer able to drive to the grocery store and didn't choose to use Meals on Wheels or arrange for alternative rides to the store, I chose to order her food online and drive her to the store occasionally.

Fill in the gaps.

Understanding that some family dynamics make these kinds of discussions impossible—you and your parents may be estranged, your father would *never* talk about his feelings and goals, your parents have already declined past the point where they could have a meaningful discussion—you may have to make some assumptions and decisions on your own. If that is the case, ask yourself these four questions and use the answers to guide you.

1. What do I know about my parents that will help inform my decision making?
2. Based on how my parents have lived their life, what do I think they value most?
3. What do I believe is best for my parents?
4. What do I believe is best for me as a caregiver?

When it was time to move my father from his assisted living apartment into a nursing home, his dementia was advanced and I couldn't talk to him about it. I had to rely on what I knew about him to make that decision. And then I had to dig deep to find the courage to balance my compassion.

ADMITTING THERE IS A PROBLEM IS THE FIRST STEP

Initiating "the conversation" requires you to acknowledge that your parents are aging, and that's not always easy. If you see them regularly, you may be slow to recognize change. Long-distance caregivers might be shocked at the changes they see each time they visit. The challenge for them is to accept that they can't make everything right in one trip. The challenge for their siblings is not to take it personally when a sibling comes to town and points out what they're observing.

Maybe you're just resistant to the idea that your parents are getting older and therefore you can't see what's in front of you. We get used to our parents being the ones we can count on and so it can be difficult to let go of that safety net. Or maybe you know that if you admit there is a problem, you're probably on the hook for dealing with it. For a long time I found it easier to be annoyed with my mother—because she walked too slow, because she stopped cooking, because she saved all of her mail for me to open and explain—than to admit she was getting older. Try to open your eyes and your mind. Planning ahead on the family front will allow you to plan ahead at work.

There are signs that can signal your parents need more help. If you notice one or more of the following, it's time to assess your parents' needs and determine if they need some lifestyle adjustments, additional support, or perhaps a change in their living situation. Likewise, it's time to determine how you can support them with the least amount of disruption to your career.

Six warning signs that your parents may need more help include the following.

Unopened or stacked mail.

Are your parents losing their handle on their bills? Is their mail piling up, unopened? Do they seem susceptible to offers in junk mail? A simple fix is to offer to help with bill paying and, if they are willing, to redirect their mail to your address. But is there a deeper issue with their cognitive ability? It may be time for a medical assessment to determine the answer to this question.

Frequent falls.

Every year, three million elderly people are treated in emergency departments for injuries related to falls.[3] And many people who fall, even if they're not injured, become afraid of falling, causing them to cut down on their everyday activities. If your parents experience a fall, it may be time for a cane or walker. If your parents are going to remain at home, evaluate their residence for trip hazards like area rugs and retrofit the bathroom with anti-slip materials and grip bars in the shower. Get a medical evaluation to check for any trauma resulting from the fall and to see if any underlying medical issues caused it.

Changes in food habits.

Have your parents stopped cooking? Is the fridge full of expired food? The kitchen can be an excellent indicator that your parents may need more support. Meals on Wheels may be an option or maybe your parents would benefit from a home health aide to prepare a few meals a week. Maybe they'd love the idea of assisted living where they can get three meals prepared for them each day. You won't know unless you ask.

Forgetfulness.

Are your parents forgetting family members' names or getting lost while traveling familiar routes? Have they left a burner on after cooking? While we often want to dismiss forgetfulness as just "old age," it's wise to have your forgetful parent assessed for cognitive decline.

Messiness.

Have you noticed your parents' home or personal appearance have become messy? This may just be a sign that they are more easily tired by household chores and could benefit from a housekeeper or a home health aide. But this could also be a sign of something more serious such as depression or dementia. Mention these signs to your parents' doctors. If you don't have a relationship with your parents' doctors and HIPPA prevents the doctors from sharing information with you, ask the doctors if they will at least listen to your input even if they can't respond to you.

Driving difficulties.

If you run errands or go out to dinner while you are visiting your parents, resist the urge to get behind the wheel and instead let your parent drive. Notice his or her reaction times, any signaling or turning issues, and any hesitation he or she may show. Is he or she no longer able or willing to drive at night? It may be time to make some alternative transportation plans for him or her like a Lyft account or a Council on Aging shuttle service.

If you do notice any of these warning signs, ask your parents how they are managing and if they have any concerns. Use open-ended questions like, "How are things going?" and "How are you managing these days?" You want to start a discussion, not tell them what they need. Listen intently and acknowledge their feelings and observations. Then you can add your observations or concerns—but be careful not to come across as judgmental or controlling.

SENIOR LIVING OPTIONS

Choosing the right living arrangements for your parents can be overwhelming. Not only are there many different choices, it can be a very emotional experience for you and your parents as you accept that they are entering a new phase of life and you go through the process of downsizing their belongings. To give you a sense of the options, here is an overview of six different types of living arrangements.

Aging in place.

This means your parents remain in their home. In order to do that they may at some point need assistance with driving, household chores, finances, bathing and dressing, and medical needs, including transportation to doctor's appointments, assistance with medication, medical tasks, physical therapy, etc., either from you, another family member, a home health aide, a visiting nurse, or some combination of people. You may also need to retrofit their home by lowering shelves, removing any trip and fall hazards such as area rugs, lowering toilet seats, and widening doors to accommodate walkers and wheelchairs.

Independent living.

These communities, often an apartment complex or cluster of cottages, allow seniors to live independently but take advantage of shared services such as dining rooms, activities, and exercise programs. If you or your parents are concerned about social isolation, a very real issue for many senior citizens, this could be a solution. Most independent living facilities are pricey, often comparable to the cost of a home, but some refund a portion of the fee after move out.

Assisted living.

Assisted living facilities differ from independent living in that residents can purchase care plans for assistance with tasks like bathing and dressing, housecleaning and laundry, and medication assistance. While assisted living facilities have nursing staff, they are not designed to provide medical attention. These facilities are not covered by Medicare or Medicaid. Some have a set number of units designated for residents in need of financial assistance and the subsidy source varies state by state. There is typically a long waiting period for subsidized units.

Memory care.

Memory care is similar to assisted living except these facilities cater to people with cognitive decline such as Alzheimer's and dementia. They offer a high level of assistance with personal care tasks plus recreational programs tailored to people with memory loss. Residents typically live in a locked area so they won't wander or get lost.

Skilled nursing facility.

A skilled nursing facility is what many of us know as a nursing home. Residents receive round the clock medical care. Most facilities have a mix of short-term and long-term residents. Short-term residents may stay there just while they receive rehabilitation services after a hospital stay.

Continuous care retirement community.

These communities, usually private pay and usually at the higher end of the cost spectrum, allow people to move into independent housing and then transfer to assisted living and/or skilled nursing as their needs increase.

A CHECKLIST FOR CHOOSING

Choosing the right facility takes thought and planning—but, like me, you don't always have the luxury of time. Remember there is no perfect solution, nor is there only one right decision. Quality of care is a major factor, but so too is availability and, quite frankly, affordability. Your job as a caregiver is to make the best possible decision based on your individual circumstances.

Here are six factors to consider when choosing the best home for your family member:

Referrals/research.

Ask around for referrals. Your parent's primary care physician, friends and relatives, staff at assisted living or a hospital, and your local Council on Aging are all possible sources of information. Then use the Nursing Home Compare tool from Medicare.gov to research safety and quality records.

Availability and cost.

If you can, start looking before you think you need to. Many facilities have long wait lists. Ask if the facility accepts Medicaid as well as private pay. Is there a different wait list depending on your method of payment? Do they require several months of private pay before accepting Medicaid?

Proximity.

Is the facility close to you and/or other family members and friends? Maybe you should choose a place close to your office so you can drop by on your lunch hour or on your way home from work. Familiar faces and frequent visits can ease your family member's transition to a new home. Can other family members easily get there so that they can visit too and give you a break when you need it? Speaking of visiting, are there set visiting hours or can you drop by any time?

Tours.

Visit the facilities you're considering and note what you see and smell. Are residents sitting in wheelchairs in the halls? Are they dressed or in hospital gowns? Is there a strong urine odor or strong chemical odor that may be masking other smells? Is there a receptionist watching the front door? Are side doors locked? Does the staff seem energetic or lethargic? Do they make eye contact and interact with residents and family members? Pro tip: Sit outside during a shift change and observe employees as they show up for work. Are they dragging or do they have some pep in their step?

Quality of life.

Can patients follow their own schedules or must they comply with routines? What activities are offered? Can you take your parent out of the facility for holidays and excursions? Do they offer services like haircuts, dental appointments, podiatry, and flu shots? Can your parent keep his or her doctor or will he or she see a facility-appointed doctor? Under what circumstances will the staff send your relative to the ER? How do they balance risk of falling with independence and autonomy? How are confusion, wandering, and behavior issues handled? What is the philosophy on psych drugs and restraining patients?

Gut check.

Sometimes the decision comes down to what your gut is telling you. Trust it.

LAWYER UP

When it comes to paying for long-term care, I cannot stress enough how useful it is to consult an elder law attorney. Yes, paying for a lawyer is an expense, but that legal fee can save you from spending or losing money you don't need to. Eldercare attorneys can help you understand your options for funding long-term care including Veteran's and Social Security benefits and how to protect your and your parents' assets. They can draw up the paperwork for power of attorney and guardianship and assist with estate planning. They can explain Medicare, the federal health insurance program for people aged sixty-five and older, which does *not* cover long-term care. And they can help you apply for Medicaid, health insurance jointly funded by states and the federal government for eligible low-income elderly adults. Many but not all nursing homes or skilled nursing facilities accept Medicaid, but often residents have to start paying from their own funds until they "spend down," or run out of, their assets. A good elder law attorney can assist you through that process. It's never too early to meet with an attorney, but know it is never too late either.

IF YOU DO MOVE A PARENT

Moving a parent, even a willing one, into a senior living facility is fraught with emotion. Your parents may mourn the loss of their younger years, their independence, and the home they built. They could be scared about aging, making new friends, and finding their way in a new place.

You may be mourning all of those things too. You may second guess your decision. Did you act too quickly? Overreact? Wait too long? You *will* feel guilt. Know that your feelings are normal and don't need to last forever.

It broke my heart to place my father in memory care. Even though the facility was less than three miles from my house, and even though I really liked the director of the memory program, I was placing my father behind a locked door with only twelve other residents, most of whom could not engage in meaningful conversation. Plus, I wasn't convinced that was where he needed to be. He wasn't either.

One night shortly after he moved in, I decided I'd stop in and say hello to him on my way home from a client meeting. It had been a productive work day, I was going to visit my father, and I would be home early enough to spend time with my kids. For a brief moment I felt like I was in control of my life. The feeling was fleeting because I found my father lying on his bed with no lights on, the look on his face as dark as his room.

"This stinks," he said. "I'm locked up against my will. I demand to know why. I don't have much time left and this is no way to live."

My heart hurt.

"Dad, you are not being held against your will. This isn't necessarily forever." I hoped I wasn't lying. "You're here because you're being assessed. You have some memory issues."

"I don't have any memory issues," he said. "How could I have run a foundry for thirty years, how could I have been responsible for high-voltage electrical equipment, if I had problems with my memory?"

"Dad, brains can change. Your brain now is not the same as your brain thirty years ago."

"Like hell it isn't. This no way to live. I don't want to be locked up with these people."

Now my heart was breaking.

I can't remember how late I stayed with him that night, but I know my kids were asleep by the time I got home. I was wrecked. And I had to get up at 6:00 the next morning because my boss was in town from California and we had an early morning meeting.

The next afternoon, I researched other facilities online, switching my computer screen to show the press release I was supposed to be working on whenever my boss walked by. After work I met with the director at my father's place to see how we could make his experience better. She offered to unlock the door to the patio so he could sit outside, even eat his meals out there, whenever he pleased. The patio had a high fence around it like the kind you see at prisons but without the barbed wire. But at least he had some fresh air.

Three days later I headed back to Cape Cod to move my mother closer to me (in the same facility where my father was locked in the memory care unit). As with many of my other parent-related trips to the Cape, I used a vacation day but still started my day before 6:00 so I could get some work done and be in the car by 9:15. I cried most of the drive; I was having a full-on pity party that day.

I pulled in to the parking lot of the assisted living home in time to host a webinar from my car that I had signed up to do months earlier. The topic? How working mothers can find balance. Oh, sweet, sweet irony.

"Where have you been?" my mother asked me when I walked into her room.

I clenched my jaw. Then she asked me what my kids were up to.

"The kids?" I said. "I haven't seen my kids in weeks. My life is all about doctors and lawyers and assisted living."

I finished packing her belongings and tried really hard to shift my mood. On the drive back, we laughed and talked and danced to the radio. By the time we arrived at my mother's new home, they were serving dinner. One of the residents, a man named Michael, asked if he could sit with us. He told my mother what a wonderful place she was moving in to.

"They have hamburgers. And ice cream. They even have ketchup. And mustard," he told her.

"I'm in hell," I thought to myself. "What I wouldn't give to be at a business dinner right now, dressed up, and ordering a great bottle of wine instead of here talking about condiments."

But my mother was thrilled. She loved her apartment and laughed about her new suitor.

On my way out, I went to see my father, worried about what I was walking into. I checked the patio first, and when I didn't see him, I assumed he was in his room brooding.

"Dad, please bear with me," I said as I entered his room. "I don't think this is the place for you but I need time."

"If you have to be stuck somewhere, this is the place to be," he responded.

Then he told me he had sung karaoke that afternoon. I pretended to call for an aide.

"Clearly you *are* crazy if you're singing in front of a crowd. I'm sending you back to the psych ward."

He laughed, but I didn't know if I should laugh or cry. They both liked it there! I couldn't keep them in the same place, could I? I'd figure that out in the morning. In the meantime it felt good to know that both of my parents were safe and happy. Maybe I did have things under control.

IT TAKES TIME

Don't underestimate what a big deal it is to move your parents to a new home. It will take time for them, and you, to adjust. One of the things caregiving teaches us is how to sit with discomfort—we don't have much choice. To help yourself through those uncomfortable transition periods, try these eleven strategies to ease the transition to senior living.

Give it time, and maybe take some time.

It can take several months for someone to adjust to senior living. If you start to think you made a bad move, wait a week or two. Stay focused on the reasons you made the decision (safety, health, security, sanity). Take a personal day or two, if you have them, during and right after the move. Your parents may need a little extra support, and you may also need some time to come to terms with the change.

Visit often, or not for two weeks.

Only you know your parent, so only you can decide how best to assist his or her through the early weeks of the move. Many experts will tell you to visit as often as possible. Frequent visits can ease any stress your parent may have that he or she will be abandoned or lonely. It might be easier for him or her to meet people at activities or in the dining room if he or she has a companion. But if your parent is calling you several times a day, staying in his or her room, and waiting for you to show up and keep him or her company, you may need to give your parent some space in order to encourage him or her to branch out. When I went to college, my parents wouldn't let me come home for the first month. By forcing me to stay at school on the weekends, they forced me to make friends. Tough love—it can work both ways.

It takes a village.

Mobilize yours. When we moved my mother into respite care, my sisters and I could not visit for a week or two. We had been staying with her before the move and we needed to get back to work. Plus, our father was in the psych ward. So I called my aunts, uncles, and cousins and asked them to visit in our absence. Just as parenting takes a village, so does daughtering.

Expect setbacks.

Just when you think you are over the hump and your parent is settling in, things will change. He or she will tell you he or she is lonely. He or she will decide he or she doesn't like his or her new dining hall friends. He or she will ask to go home. These moments are heart wrenching but knowing that they are normal and that they will pass can help get you through them.

Acknowledge the difficult parts.

Yes, you want to paint the new move in a positive light, but don't talk *at* your parents about all the wonderful new activities and people and opportunities. Listen to their fears and concerns and acknowledge them. Then help them get through it. They will be more likely to listen to what you have to say if they feel like you've listened to what they had to say.

Surround your parents with their personal belongings.

Moving to senior living usually means downsizing. The maple dining room table with two extension leaves may not fit in the new apartment. But what does fit are photographs of family and friends, favorite books, a familiar piece of artwork. If you need to downsize the bedroom set, you can still bring a familiar blanket and pillows. The kitchen may be new, but you can pack your mother's favorite teacup. Leaving a home shouldn't mean leaving behind the comforts of that home.

Limit new things.

You may be tempted to furnish your parent's new place with the latest and greatest in hopes he or she loves his or her fancy new home. But limit new items. Moving into senior living is a major adjustment where everything is new—the people, the food, the routines. Don't overwhelm your parent with a new phone or even a new coffee maker. Limit the number of new things he or she needs to learn how to operate.

Be your parent's advocate.

No place is perfect. You and your parent may see opportunities to improve something at his or her new home, but your parent may hesitate to speak up when he or she moves to a new place. If that is the case, do it for him or her. When my father moved to the assisted living area, he liked to sit outside on a second-floor porch until well after midnight. The aides kept insisting he go inside. So I asked management why he couldn't stay out late. It turned out the staff just wasn't used to seeing residents out of their rooms after 8:30.

Build a team.

The staff should be a part of your team. Talk to them about your concerns and your parent's concerns and actively enroll them in helping with the transition. Don't assume they will notice what needs to happen—they are very busy. If your parent tells you he or she is too shy to go to the dining hall for dinner or he or she forgets when activities are happening, ask if a staff member can knock on his or her door and invite him or her. If the staff members know what you need, they should be willing to help out.

Set your boundaries.

Yes, you want to be a good daughter and ease your parent's transition. But you have needs too. Try to free up as much time as you can in the first few months after the move to help ease the transition but know that it is okay if you are not always available. Your kids may need you. Your boss and co-workers may need you. And you need to take care of yourself. Determine what you are able and willing to do and then stick to your boundaries. Other people will tell you what you should do. Ignore them. There are no shoulds.

Remember daughter knows best.

Staff and other well-meaning people may tell you to stay away or visit often. They may tell you to dismiss complaints as normal. But you know your parent best. Trust your instincts. I knew my father didn't belong in a locked memory care unit, but when I expressed my doubts about that decision, his doctors and social workers dismissed me as a daughter in denial. I persisted and a few weeks after his hospital discharge his memory improved and confusion went away. It turned out that a urinary tract infection had caused delirium. So after my mother moved to a hospice home, he moved into his own apartment on the assisted living side of the facility and he was able to stay there for three years until his dementia advanced.

THE CASE FOR SEPARATE BATHROOMS

Moving a parent in with you, or moving in with a parent, is as big of a deal as moving your parent to senior living; the challenges are just different. Abby, a single woman in her early fifties, decided to bring her mother to live with her, in a different state, after her father passed away. "I knew I wanted to do the right thing," she told me, "But I didn't know how to get it done."

Her mother had high blood pressure, diabetes, and only partial mobility on her left side after suffering a stroke. Abby had to find a doctor, buy a hospital bed, rip up her carpeting and install laminate floors so that her mother's wheelchair would glide easily, remove her tub and install a shower stall with a seat, put grab rails in the bathroom, and have all of the doorways in the house widened. "While I was at it, I had the contractor build a granite top wet bar—just for me."

She got a lesson in how to change an adult diaper, a lesson in how to transfer someone from a wheelchair to a bed, and she hired aides to stay with her mother when she was at work. "I interviewed forty-five CNAs [certified nursing assistants]" she said. "Only six were keepers."

The hardest part, she says, was realizing that she would be providing care every day.

Here are five tips for living with a parent.

Remember who the adult is.

You both are! Your parents may be living under your roof, but don't treat them like children. You may be living with your parents, maybe you even moved back to the house, perhaps even the bedroom, where you grew up, but you are not a child anymore. You don't need permission to stay out all night—and neither do they. Before the move, talk about the boundaries each of you want to set. Will you check in when you are running late? Will you tell each other where you are going, when you are leaving, and when you'll be home? Will you cook together or take turns? How will they interact with your children? Does your parent have permission to reprimand your child? How about spoiling them?

Build in daughter time.

If your parent needs assistance with dressing, bathing, and eating or if you are managing his or her medication and handling other medical tasks, try to set aside some time each week to be a daughter and not just a nurse. Maybe there's a television show you watch together every week, or you plan a weekly outing, or carve out twenty minutes every morning just to talk. It can be very difficult to find that extra time, but preserving your relationship will be worth it.

Carve out private space and time.

Just because you're cohabitating doesn't mean you have to do everything together. Designate an area of the house where you can each go for privacy. Every working daughter I know who lives with a parent tells me this is key. Designate your own quiet time too. Don't be afraid to tell your parent that your morning coffee time is sacred or you don't want company watching *The Late Show*. And don't be offended if they tell you the same. Explain up front that there may be times you need to work at home—joining conference calls or trying to meet deadlines—and when that happens you can only be interrupted for true emergencies. And pro tip from every working daughter I know who lives with a parent: Have separate bathrooms if possible.

Discuss the finances.

Determine if, and how, you will share expenses. Will you each contribute to grocery and utility bills? Will you live in your parents' home rent free in exchange for your care? Will your arrangement impact their will in any way? Moving in together is a great time to consult an elder law attorney. You will want to understand how to protect each of your assets and how to execute whatever agreement you come up with.

Be open to changes.

No one gets younger. Your parents may be fairly independent when they move in but require more care and attention over time. Be prepared to rethink your agreements and arrangements as they age.

The bottom line is this: only you and your siblings, if they are involved in your parents' care, your partner if you have one, and the person you care for, with input from health professionals and senior care specialists, can determine what is best for your family. Remember, as with parenting, there is no one right answer. The best decisions and outcomes will stem from a clear head, an open heart, and a guilt-free conscience. And you should never feel guilty for doing your best, even when your best is imperfect.

Chapter Six

Manage

"I don't want you talking and driving, Liz." Peg, the hospice nurse, wanted me to call her back when I had a few minutes to talk. Because that would most likely be never, I lied and told her I had pulled over to the side of the road and turned the car engine off. It was only Monday but I was already fried.

I had set my alarm for 5:00 that morning because I had so much to do, but I didn't get out of bed until 7:30. The San Francisco team at work was supposed to have sent me a report to review and send to our client but it wasn't in my inbox. I could feel my stress; it felt like a band around my heart. I sent an email asking the team to send it ASAP but I would have to wait hours before they even got to work. So I passed the time by filling out some paperwork for our company CFO, responding to a few emails, and typing up some notes.

Then I started on parent-related tasks. I needed to cash out my parents' annuity in order to pay their rent to the assisted living facility. It was due on Friday. In order to make the payment, I needed my mother to sign a form from the bank, which the bank was supposed to have faxed to me the day before but hadn't (a common occurrence that week), as well as papers giving me power of attorney, all of which I had to deliver to my lawyer in the city. The band around my chest tightened. I left a message for the bank representative to please call before noon. My plan was to have my mother sign her form, drop the paperwork at the lawyer, and then get to the coworking space I sometimes worked from by 2 o'clock.

It seemed like I rarely showered anymore—no time—but I had to that morning as I had a client meeting scheduled for the end of the day. While I was washing my hair, I could hear my cell phone ringing. "This is my life now," I thought. "Constant ringing and buzzing." But still no call from the bank.

So I called Verizon while I waited. I was trying to reduce my mother's bill because I was spending so much of my parents' money moving them to the senior living facility and hiring an elder law attorney and I didn't have a handle on how far I could stretch their finances. Unfortunately, I had to hang up before I spoke to a human because the bank finally called me back. The representative told me he was faxing the forms but he would not be able to get me a check by Friday. The band was around my throat now and I feared it would choke me. It was already 11:45. My client emailed me to ask me where the document was and I started to cry. I thought this must be what death by a thousand paper cuts feels like, and then I thought, I don't have time to cry.

I emailed my coworkers again, instructing them to please send the report directly to the client. *I am going offline for a few hours. If you have questions, call my cell,* I wrote. A few minutes later, the assistant wrote back. *Who do you want to do this?* I pounded the keyboard as I responded. *Sorry if I was unclear. I am logging off. I won't read email again until 2PM ET and we need to get the report to the client before then. Can you please send? I really appreciate it. Thanks.* But actually, I didn't appreciate it at all.

I drove to my mother's, practically shoved the papers and a pen in her face, and then I headed to the city. That's when Peg called.

"I examined your mother this morning," she told me, "and she appears to have a mass obstructing her intestine. I think she needs more care than you and I can give her in assisted living. I think she would be better off in a hospice home."

I made a mental note to add "buy funeral clothes for the kids" and "write eulogy" to my to-do list.

The following weekend I went to the Cape to spend time with my husband and kids. I didn't want to go at first and I argued with my husband about it. The oncologist I had met with the week before said he would visit my mother. She had fluid around her lungs and he had offered to examine her and see if he could help relieve some of the pressure. I told my husband I wanted to be there. Plus, I just didn't have the energy to pack an overnight bag.

Kevin left for the Cape early Saturday morning with the kids, clearly miffed. He thought it was important that we spend some time as a family and didn't think I needed to stay home for the doctor's visit. I watched him drive away, frustrated that he didn't understand what I was going through. Then I cried for a little while and called him on his cell.

"I just don't know what to do," I said. I was starting to experience what psychologists call anticipatory grief. Some people mourn when they are expecting the death of someone they are close to, and the feelings can be very similar to the grief we experience after someone has passed away. But I didn't know how to articulate this.

"Do what you think is right," he said.

His words were deliberate; he was leaving it up to me to interpret what he meant. I could hear them as a guilt trip or as permission to stay home. His tone, however, conveyed a clear meaning. "Whatever Liz. I'm done talking about this."

As I accepted my mother's prognosis—three months to live—and started to grieve, I grew more and more protective of her and felt the need to direct as much of her care as I possibly could. Professors from the University of Calgary published a research paper examining the strategies family members use to prepare themselves for a loved one's death. "Emotional processes such as protection and intense involvement in every-day caregiving throughout the illness assured families that care and comfort were given to their loved one."[1] I had always been a control freak, and now I was doubling down on those tendencies. Looking back, my actions made sense, but that morning I didn't understand my own feelings; I only knew they were primal.

Deep down I knew I couldn't control what happened to my mother. Cancer makes its own rules. So I decided I would join my family after all. I did need to invest some time with my kids, and a few hours on the beach in the company of my aunts, uncles, and cousins was good for my soul. I sent an email to the doctor. *In an effort to keep my family from imploding, I am heading to the Cape. If you want to visit my mother feel free.* Then I packed a bag and hopped in the car.

As I drove along in bumper-to-bumper summer vacation traffic—there was an eleven-mile backup at the Cape Cod Canal—I thought about my mother. I remembered how she used to play dodgeball with my sisters and me in the driveway after dinner. I thought about her sense of humor and all the silly songs she taught us about cannibal kings and flying purple people eaters. I remembered the grace and strength she exhibited when she was diagnosed with a brain tumor twenty years earlier. I thought about just how much I loved her and how much she mattered to me. And feeling both nostalgia for my childhood and anxiety about being stuck in gridlock when I had such a lengthy to-do list, I wrote her eulogy, right there in my car, dictating into the Notes app on my iPhone.

That summer, and for a while after my parents were diagnosed, I thought I was special. One woman juggling it all! Two terminal diagnoses! Three business trips to fit in! Four hospitalizations! Five moves in two months! I vacillated between thinking, "Omigod, this is going to break me," and "Omigod, I am superhuman. A lesser being would crack under this pressure." But it turns out that I was not alone, nor were my circumstances that extraordinary.

NEVERTHELESS, SHE PERSISTED

I've since met Marnie, who is caring for her mother who has cancer and her father who has Parkinson's, while she runs her own business. I've met Juanita, who gave up her own career to care for her bedridden mother and her father with heart disease and took over running her parents' business. I have met hundreds of working daughters who are dealing with just as much stress and responsibility as I did, and in many cases much, much more. Like me, they had no warning, no training, and very little, if any, support. They faced challenges daily but they persisted and are managing their situations skillfully. And that's the key: managing. The working daughters I meet who are doing more than hanging on, who are thriving instead of merely surviving, take an active approach to caregiving and to balancing their family responsibilities with their jobs.

There is so much you cannot control as a working daughter. You can't control illness; you can only provide the best care possible. You can't control someone else's aging process. Heck, outside of moisturizer, hair dye, and fillers, you can't really control your own aging either. All you can do is manage the best you can and control what you can control.

No matter what stage of caregiving you are in right now—providing light support, worrying about the future, navigating a full-blown crisis, or staving off long-term burnout—take a proactive approach and manage the things you can manage. Lean in to your caregiving role. Trust me, it beats the alternative—ignoring, worrying, and then scrambling. As singer/songwriter Joan Baez once said, "Action is the antidote to despair."

Here are four key aspects of eldercare where you can take action.

1. HEALTH

Your job, as it relates to your parents' health, is first and foremost to be their advocate. In order to do that, you need to understand what kind of care your parents wish to receive and make sure you have access to the information you will need to support them.

Doctors

Buy a hardcover notebook, small enough to fit in a purse, and record the following information in it: the name of your parent's primary care physician (PCP), the phone number, and the name of the practice. The PCP should serve as the first line of contact for your parent's medical issues and help coordinate with specialists and hospitalists when necessary. Some older adults see a geriatrician, a doctor who specializes in the elderly, as their primary care. While this expertise is quite helpful, a PCP who understands the unique needs of older adults can also be sufficient.

Also make note of the names and phone numbers of any specialists that your parent either sees or is referred to. This can include cardiologists, oncologists, pulmonary experts, podiatrists, etc. If your parent receives any nursing support at home, make sure to include the name and number of the coordinating agency and the visit schedule. Store all of this information electronically as well. Ideally, you want to establish a line of communication with all of the medical professionals who treat your parent. We'll talk more about how to be an effective advocate in chapter 7. But to start, you need to have permission to receive information about your parent's health, and that involves filling out the right paperwork.

Paperwork

The paperwork you need in order to be your parent's health advocate includes the following.

Healthcare proxy aka Durable Medical Power of Attorney.

Your parents should each designate one person to be their health care proxy. This person, often the primary caregiver, has the authority to make medical decisions for a patient in the event he or she is unable to. Some people have a proxy statement prepared by an attorney, while others complete a form at their doctor's office or at the hospital. Most proxies require at least two witnesses to sign them, but requirements vary state by state. Also proxies can be changed, so if, for example, your parent names someone who can no longer fulfill the role, he or she can assign someone else. When you are a proxy, doctors will share information with you. If you are not the proxy, doctors are not allowed to discuss a patient's medical issues with you due to the Health Insurance Portability and Accountability Act of 1996, commonly known as HIPAA. Pro tip: Some hospitals only recognize a proxy form completed at their facility and some only accept original copies. Therefore, if you are your parent's proxy, always keep your original form as well as a few copies with you. Do not trust that a hospital or medical practice shares proxy information across different departments. Without this document, you cannot speak about or make medical decisions for your parent.

Advanced directive aka living will.

An advanced directive, sometimes referred to as a living will or physician orders for life-sustaining treatment (POLST), clearly spells out what, if any, medical intervention your parent wants to receive in certain medical situations in the event that he or she cannot communicate his or her preference. In some states, a patient can complete an advanced directive with his or her primary care physician. These directives cover whether or not a patient would want a feeding tube, for example, if he or she were unable to eat, or the use of life-sustaining treatments such as ventilators and heart-lung machines. Again, patients can update these directives if their wishes change. Advanced directives may be unpleasant to think about and discuss, but they can provide clarity and peace of mind for a caregiver in a difficult situation.

When my father was in his late eighties, together with his primary care physician and me, he made the decision that he would never have surgery, except perhaps if he broke a hip or bone and was in pain. Years later, I had to bring him to the emergency room because he had an infection that was not responding to antibiotics. A surgeon came in and told me he was going to operate. When I told him, "No. Give me some other options," he was indignant and made it clear he thought I was wrong. Alone at 3:30 in the morning, I started to question myself. If not for that advance directive, doubt and exhaustion might have convinced me to let the surgeon cut open a ninety-one-year-old man with dementia. Pro tip: If your parents are very ill, consider posting their advanced directive above their bed so nursing home staff, EMTs, or other responders will see it during an emergency.

DNR.

DNR stands for Do Not Resuscitate. This can be a doctor's order or a legal document that tells medical staff not to perform cardiopulmonary resuscitation (CPR) or advanced cardiac life support in the event a patient stops breathing or his or her heart stops. A DNR can be part of an advanced directive or a person could opt to have just a DNR without an advanced directive. You may hear the term "Allow Natural Death" in place of DNR. Some medical professionals are advocating the use of this phrase in place of DNR as it better defines the decision a patient and/or his or her proxy is making.

Other information you need in order to manage health concerns includes a medication list with the name, dose, and time of every medication your parent takes—even better if you also list why he or she takes it, contact information for the pharmacy, a copy (front and back) of his or her insurance cards, and a medical history. Use the following checklist to put together a complete record of your parent's medical history.

- Full name
- Date of birth
- Blood type
- Allergies
- Primary care physician (name and phone)

- Other doctors currently providing care (name and phone)
- Last flu shot
- Existing health problems
- Past surgeries (with dates)
- Past hospitalizations (dates and reasons)
- External aids (eyeglasses, hearing aids, cane, walker, dentures)
- Dentist (name and phone)
- Organ donor (yes or no)

Keep copies of all of this information in three different places: your home, your office, and your glove compartment. That way, if you are taking your parent to the doctor or if there is an emergency, no matter where you are, you will have what you need. Pro tip: Take pictures of insurance cards, medication lists, any current lab results, etc. and keep them on your smart phone as backup.

Obtaining, organizing, and accessing the right paperwork will make medical appointments more efficient, and preparing for them in advance will make them more productive.

Here are seven ways to make your parent's doctor's appointment productive.

Schedule strategically.

Minimize wait times by either booking the first appointment of the day or the first appointment after lunch. It's less likely the doctor will be running late at these times.

Pad your time.

Plan buffer time. Try to plan an extra hour or better yet ninety minutes for the appointment. Thinking you only need to take two hours off of work for a one-hour appointment is what I call magical thinking. And magical thinking is a working daughter's enemy. Your parent may not be ready when you go to pick him or her up. He or she may move slower than you'd like. The doctor may send him or her for tests. Plan for the worst and hope for the best. Why set yourself up for frustration and stress?

Use email.

Ask the doctor's office to email you any forms you will need to fill out in advance of your appointment. Doctor's offices don't typically see you based on appointment time, they see you based on when you arrive in the office. For example, if you have an 11 o'clock appointment but arrive before the person who is booked for 10:30, you will probably be called in ahead of him or her. If you arrive with your paperwork already completed, it may bump you up on the waiting room list. Bonus: If you establish an email correspondence with your parent's doctor's office, you can cut down on the number of personal calls you have to take at work. If you have a question or want to make or change an appointment, send an email. No one will need to know you're handling a caregiving task at work.

Agree on priorities.

Here's a common scenario among caregivers: Your parent asks you to make an appointment due to some specific ailment. But when the doctor walks in and asks why he or she is there, your parent says, "I have no idea," and throws a particularly shady glance your way. You feel your pulse quicken wondering why you're missing work again if your mother isn't even going to admit she's not feeling well. It happened to me more times than I care to remember. Talk with your parent before the visit. Agree on what the goals are for the appointment. You and your parent may not stick to the plan, but you will accomplish more having thought through the visit than if you just wing it.

Use diplomacy.

If you want to give input at the appointment, frame your thoughts as observations. "What I've observed" is much less accusatory and threatening to your parent than "My mother forgets everything."

Take notes.

Take notes *during* the visit on your smart phone or in your notebook, not after the visit. Read the notes back to the doctor or nurse before the visit ends to make sure you captured what you need to remember.

Bring a list of questions and concerns.

Keep track of questions and concerns as you think of them on your smart phone so you can access them when you are at the doctor. Too many caregivers think, "I'll definitely remember to ask that," and let's face it, you probably don't even remember what you had for breakfast this morning, do you? Ask your parent what his or her concerns are and add those to the list too. This is his or her appointment after all.

In addition to your own list of questions and concerns, here are some additional questions you may want to ask.

1. What changes and symptoms should I report as I observe them?

2. What should trigger a call to the doctor or to 911?
3. What possible side effects should we expect from medication?
4. Can we reevaluate his or her medication list? Can any prescriptions or doses be changed, reduced, or removed?

2. FINANCIAL/LEGAL

"We have Harry." My mother and I would stick our noses in the air and say this when we were filling out legal documents in the last months of her life. We were bragging about our elder law attorney. Right after my parents were diagnosed, a friend texted me. *How can I help? What do you need?* My reply was sarcastic because I was so overwhelmed I didn't think anyone could help. *I need to find a memory care place for my Dad by Friday, I need a lawyer and a trip to a spa. Can you help?* I should have known that she could; this friend is one of the most networked women I know. While she didn't book me into Canyon Ranch, she did send me a sparkly necklace to cheer me up and she referred me to her friend who in turn referred me to an attorney. I didn't know at the time that he was a recognized expert in elder law. One day a few weeks later, my mother mentioned this attorney's name to one of the directors at the assisted living facility and the woman, clearly impressed, exclaimed, "Wow. You have Harry? How'd you get him?"

Caregivers are often called on to manage their parents' finances and personal affairs. This can be a daunting but critical task. I stated this earlier, but it bears repeating: hiring an elder law attorney is a one of the smartest things you can do to help you plan for your parents' later years. Elder law attorneys can assist with a number of things including health directives, creating guardianships, writing wills, and guiding families through any disagreements related to assets and inheritance. To find an attorney, ask around for referrals—you might get a "Harry"—and/or visit the National Elder Law Foundation (NELF) website (www.nelf.org), an organization that certifies attorneys specializing in elder and special needs law.

Prior to working with an attorney, you might want to work with a financial planner to organize your parents' finances, or yours if you will be providing financial support, and advise you on how best to meet short- and long-term financial goals.

Of course, sometimes paying for expertise is just not possible. Know that plenty of working daughters manage their parents' finances and long-term care planning on their own. Regardless of whether or not you work with a financial or legal advisor, here are some items you should consider.

Public benefits.

Your parent may be eligible for aid, either based on his or her income, age, military service, or for a host of other reasons. These benefits, which vary by state, can help with a variety of expenses from medication to food to taxes to utilities. The AARP Foundation offers an overview of benefits and how to access them on their website (www.aarp.org/quicklink). Most municipalities also have a Department of Elder Affairs or a Council on Aging that should be able to help. Pro tip: Call these departments and agencies and schedule an appointment versus searching their websites. Government agency websites, with some exceptions, are often dense, poorly organized, and frustrating as hell. Bite the bullet and find the time for a face-to-face meeting.

Veteran's benefits.

According to a 2012 U.S. Census brief, there are approximately twelve million U.S. veterans aged sixty-five or older.[2] If your parents served, they may be eligible for benefits and services from the Department of Veterans Affairs (VA). In addition to healthcare-related services, other available benefits may include financial aid in the form of a monthly pension based on whether the veteran lives in a nursing home or is housebound. For the most updated services available and for application forms, visit the Department of Veteran Affairs website (www.va.org). Pro tip: The application for veteran's benefits is complex, but most municipalities have a veteran's affairs officer. Contact this person for help filing and completing forms. I made an appointment with my local officer and showed up with my Dad and his Army discharge papers. The officer filled out my father's application, filed it, and a few months later, my father started receiving support.

Power of attorney and guardianship.

Your parents may designate you or someone else they trust to be their power of attorney (POA). This designation allows you to handle financial and legal affairs on their behalf. You can help pay bills, talk to insurance agents, and sign legal documents for your parents. Suggesting your parents give you that kind of access may feel awkward, but having POA is a godsend if your parents become unable to manage their own accounts. And like a medical power of attorney or a proxy, they can change their mind and revoke POA. Different from a POA, a guardian is someone a court appoints to manage another person's welfare. Some adult children seek guardianship because their parents did not have a POA in place and they are unable to care for themselves or make healthy and safe decisions. The process for securing guardianship varies by state but typically involves filing an application in probate court. Pro tip: Have a lawyer make multiple original copies of your

POA paperwork as many institutions require an original copy and you will not want to give away your only one.

Paying for long-term care.

In a 2017 report, professional services firm PwC estimates that the average lifetime cost of long-term care is $172,000 per person and that costs are expected to grow "enormously" over the next few decades.[3] The same report also found that funding for long-term care typically comes from one or more of four sources: personal savings, insurance, financial support from family, and Medicaid. A parent outliving his or her assets is a very real possibility. Remember, Medicare, the federal health insurance program for people aged sixty-five and older, does not cover long-term care, and Medicaid eligibility is based on income level. Many people discover that their parents have too many assets to qualify for Medicaid but not enough to sustain them for many years. And of course, many parents want to protect their assets either for a spouse or to pass on to their children. This is where a professional can be valuable because they can guide your family through the available options. And if you can't afford to hire a professional to assist you, you can still get help. I found the business managers at the different facilities my parents lived in to be very willing to help me understand payment options and financing plans. Also check local senior centers and Councils on Aging as many of them offer free legal and financial workshops.

Wills and estate planning.

Without a will, your parents have no say over how their assets are distributed after they die. Instead the laws of the state where they reside dictate distribution. In most cases property and valuables are given to a surviving spouse, to children, or perhaps to surviving siblings, depending on the state's laws of succession. It doesn't matter if everyone in the family knew that your parents wanted their grandson to have their car or one of their children to have their condo; if they don't have a will, you may not be able to honor their wishes. Besides a will, other estate planning issues you and your parents may want to consider include naming a guardian for any dependents they may have, providing for family members in need of care, securing life insurance to cover burial costs, and dissolving or selling a family business if they owned one.

In addition to my parents' will, my mother had notes about how she wanted her few pieces of jewelry divided among her three daughters. They were written on the same piece of yellow lined paper where she had noted her funeral plans. One night when she was in the hospice house, she asked me to bring her jewelry box to her. "Elizabeth," she said, "I want to go over who gets what."

She handed me the rings she wanted each of my sisters to have. But the ring she wanted me to have, her wedding band, was still on her finger. About a week later, one of the hospice nurses met me at the door of the home. I was stopping by for a brief visit with my mother on my way to my coworking space.

"Your mother's hand is swollen and her wedding ring is cutting into her finger. I think she should go to the ER so they can remove it. Can you go with her?"

I didn't have any calls scheduled until after lunch, but I was planning to use the morning to write monthly status reports for my clients. Now I would have to work late—again—to complete them.

In the ER, several nurses tried twisting the ring off, but it wouldn't budge. "We need to cut it," one of them told us.

"Omigod, it figures." I couldn't pass on the opportunity to tease my mother.

"What?" she said.

"Haven't I been doing enough? And now even the gift you're giving me is going to require me to do something. Rita and Eileen don't have to bring their rings to the jeweler to be repaired. You just keep piling it on with me."

She laughed.

One of the nurses came in carrying what looked like oversize wire cutters and he snipped the ring right through the inscription on the inside of the band. I felt a lump suddenly rise in my throat and my eyes welled with tears. It was as if he was cutting our family apart. Then he put the ring in a urine sample cup and handed it to me. I, on the other hand, wrapped my sisters' rings in tissue paper and gift bags to give them on the day of my mother's funeral.

Everyday bills and life maintenance.

In addition to some of the complex issues you may need to tackle as a working daughter, there are a number of more mundane, but equally important, pieces of information that you should gather to help you manage your role. Here's a checklist of information you should have so that you can support your parents:

- Bank accounts
- Life insurance policies
- Homeowner's insurance policy
- Name and number of their insurance agent
- Social Security numbers
- Information on any pensions or annuities they may have
- Safety deposit box (location, number, key)

- Mortgages and deeds
- List of monthly bills including utilities

3. LIFESTYLE

As Joseph F. Coughlin, director of the MIT AgeLab and author of *The Longevity Economy*, said in an interview with MIT News, "Our challenge is to ensure quality of life, for a century of life."[4] He's right. As science contributes to longer life spans, society needs to examine what it takes for people to remain active and engaged for longer.

But society is not tackling this issue fast enough, and for many working daughters it falls solely on them to help their parents maintain quality of life, and it is one the most difficult aspects of eldercare to manage. Medical issues are mostly nonnegotiable. If your parent needs care, you make it happen. And as stressful as it can be to have to ask for time off from work to take your mother to her cardiology appointment, it's even more stressful to contemplate taking time away from work so you can drive her to play mahjong. With financial and legal issues, there are guidelines and rules that aid you in executing a plan. But with lifestyle issues—making sure your parents are socializing, driving them places if they no longer drive, visiting them, getting them out of the house and exercising—it seems there is always more you could be doing to improve their quality of life.

Working mothers with means often "throw money at the problem" of work life balance. They hire nannies or utilize daycare to buy time so that they can go to work. But for working daughters it's not so easy. Parents are not children with little or no say in their care, they are adults with autonomy. You cannot insist that they allow an aid or an elder companion into their home to help them. And as frustrating as it can be when they don't accept help from others, it is also understandable. Eldercare, after all, is not just a series of tasks that can be delegated. At its core, eldercare is a profound act of love.

So the best way to manage this aspect of caregiving without sacrificing your sleep and jeopardizing your job is to set boundaries for yourself. Think about not just your parents' needs but your needs too. Refer to your list of nonnegotiables and make sure you put the structures in place to protect them. And the next time you're struggling with whether or not to raise your hand for a plum assignment at work or take on an extra shift, refer to the Working Daughter Bill of Rights and remind yourself:

- You have the right to a life. Nowhere is it written that family caregivers must shelve their own lives to manage someone else's. You have a right to maintain your relationships and personal interests. Carve out time for you. If others don't approve, then don't approve of their opinion.

- You have the right to set boundaries. You have the right to balance your own needs with the needs of the people you care for. Know your personal limits and say no to requests that push those limits.
- You have the right to earn a living. Even though society relies heavily and unfairly on women to do the unpaid work of care, women deserve the right to earn a living. You have the right to a job and even a career. It is not only your right, it is smart to have an income source and a plan for your own retirement and future care needs. You never need to apologize for working.
- You have the right to ask for and receive help. You have the right to accept that you cannot do everything. You have the right to ask for support from siblings, extended family members, friends, social workers, doctors, etc. And you have the right to say, "Yes, thank you," when you hear the words, "Can I do anything to help?"
- You have the right to be healthy. No one else's health should supersede your own. You have the right to sleep, eat, exercise, and do whatever else is needed to protect your physical and mental health. You will be a better caregiver if you care for yourself.
- You have the right to be good enough. You have the right to let the laundry pile high, leave the dirty dishes in the sink, and leave the bed unmade. You have the right to wear yoga pants seven days a week. You have the right to serve your children cereal for dinner, again. You can kick perfection to the curb and settle for good enough.

4. END OF LIFE

Surprisingly, one of the easier aspects of eldercare to manage is end-of-life planning. It is prudent to think about, and ask, how your parents will want to be memorialized and buried after they die. That's because funeral planning is not unlike planning a wedding—it's expensive, there are lots of little details (more than one hundred[5]), guest lists can be tricky, and emotions run high.

If the idea of talking to your parents about their funeral makes you uncomfortable, you are not alone. Americans in general are uncomfortable even thinking about death.[6] So how best to raise the issue? Unfortunately, there's no perfect approach. The answer is it depends on your relationship with your parents, their frame of mind, and your family dynamics. Some possible conversation starters are, "I hope you know this is the last thing I want to face but," or, "It is important to me that I honor your wishes. Can we talk about . . . ," or, "I hope you don't mind me asking, but is there anything I need to know about your end-of-life wishes or plans?"

Maybe your parent wants to be cremated or buried next to a certain family member. Maybe he or she already purchased a burial plot. You need to know these things! You will also want to know where he or she keeps his or her close friends' phone numbers or email addresses so you can notify them of the services when the time comes. And if your parent moves into a hospice or nursing home at some point, somewhere in the piles of paperwork you will have to fill out you will be asked if you have a preference for a funeral home.

THE DEVIL IS IN THE DETAILS

I didn't understand until after she was gone what a gift my mother gave me in sharing her funeral plans with me. And even still I managed to overcomplicate things. I knew the funeral director and knew that he was making arrangements with the church. I knew what music my mother wanted and where she would be buried. My kids had decent clothes to wear to the services thanks to my cousin who took them shopping. But what I didn't know was when and where to have a reception for friends and family because the church and the cemetery were sixty miles apart.

I called my sisters the morning after my mother died to discuss options with them. One of them was running errands and said she couldn't talk. The other didn't answer but she did text me later. *Do whatever you want. I just want to show up and not think about it.* Some of my aunts and cousins more than made up for the opinions my sisters lacked. I got all kinds of advice. Have the reception at home. Have it on the Cape. Have it soon. Have it later. Have a breakfast. Have a lunch. I was in overdrive, spinning from all of the options but wanting to make a decision immediately. I decided I would invite people to my house after the wake and then host a brunch the next day in between the church service and the burial. In hindsight, it was too much, but that day I just wanted to check things off of my to-do list. Before noon I had called a caterer, rented a hall for the brunch, picked out flowers, and hopped in my car to bring my mother's burial outfit to the funeral home.

Underwear! I had the dress, the shoes, the necklace, and the earrings, but I had forgotten to bring her any underwear! She and I had agreed that she wouldn't wear panty hose in heaven, but I knew she would not want to go commando. So I took a detour to TJ Maxx. I must have been suffering from decision fatigue because I stood for almost twenty minutes in the lingerie department trying to decide between a leopard pattern bikini and a pair of granny whites. Only my mother knows what I decided to buy and she took that information to her grave—literally.

DON'T FORGET SUNSCREEN

A few years later, when my Dad died, I was better prepared and I managed every detail of his funeral like a pro. I scheduled a simple graveside service on Cape Cod followed by lunch at one of my father's favorite spots on the water and I didn't consult anyone about the plans.

The day we buried him was gorgeous summer—sunny and in the high seventies, the sky a cornflower blue with a few fluffy clouds. After lunch most of my father's family went to the beach. As she was leaving, one of my cousins said to me, "You know it's a great funeral when you pack a suit." A bathing suit that is.

Chapter Seven

Disrupt

"My father is not going to die in that place." I was sobbing on the phone to my cousin's friend's husband. My father was in another psychiatric ward, and I was trying to get him out. I was desperate, calling anyone that I thought could help me.

After he was hospitalized for an infection, my father was sent to a short-term rehab facility. The first night there, he couldn't figure out how to use the call button, got up by himself, fell, and was sent back to the emergency room. I met him there at 3 a.m. and drove him back to the rehab in time to get home and drive my kids to school. Then I napped for a few hours before I logged onto my computer sometime around 10:30 to work. The second night he woke up in the middle of the night, disoriented, and demanded to be released. When the staff told him he couldn't leave, he tried to smash the window open with a fire extinguisher and insisted they call the police. As the son of a police captain, I suspect that in his confused state, he thought the police officer who showed up would be someone who worked for his father and would be able to vouch for him. But the officer who responded deemed my father a danger to himself and others and had him sent to a different hospital—one with a geriatric psych unit. For the second night in a row, my sleep was disrupted when my cell phone rang from under my pillow where I placed it so that I wouldn't miss an emergency call. And for the second night in a row, I rushed off to meet my father at a hospital.

The doctor in the ER told me he was going to admit my father. I didn't like the idea of hospitalizing him and it wasn't clear to me what he was being admitted for, but I didn't think I could send him back to the rehab and I knew he would need round the clock supervision in his assisted living apartment. I stayed with him until a nurse wheeled him to a room, sometime around 4 a.m. I needed to go home, cancel my reservations on the Acela train—I was supposed to go to New York for work that morning—email my boss to let her know I wouldn't be going, get some sleep, and then wake up and make a plan. For the second day in a row, my work day would be disrupted too.

GET ME OUT OF HERE

Sometime around noon I went back to the hospital, put my purse and cell phone in a locker per a notice on the door to the ward, and rang a bell to be let in. The unit was bleak. There was a desk with a plexiglass partition to the right and a room with a television blaring to the left. Someone had stuck fish decals on the walls as decorations. A few patients walked by, their johnnies untied and their backsides exposed.

A nurse told me she would bring my father to me as visitors were not allowed in patients' rooms. I was shocked when I saw him, in a t-shirt and hospital pants, strapped down in his wheelchair and slumped over. The nurse wheeled him into the TV room where my father and I tried talking, but the TV was too loud. When I told the nurse she shrugged.

"You can sit in the sun room."

It sounded promising, but it was merely a dingy room with windows. My father tried to stand up and look outside. When he realized he was strapped down to his chair, he became agitated.

"Get me out of here Liz," he pleaded.

"I will, Dad. I just need to figure out what's going on."

There was a social worker named Cody on the floor and he invited me into his office, which was barely bigger than a broom closet.

"What's the plan?" I asked.

"The doctor saw your father this morning. He'll be back tomorrow if you have any questions."

"Tomorrow? I have questions now. Why is my father staying here?"

"I'm sure the doctor can answer your questions tomorrow."

"I don't even know who this doctor is and I am my father's health care proxy. Why didn't he call me? I'm not going to wait until tomorrow to find out what's going on. Someone should have called me."

Cody told me the doctor was excellent; he had been working with him for a long time. I just stared at him. Did he really think that was good enough for me to leave my father in his care? "Let me give you his office number," Cody said.

Because I couldn't bring any personal belongings onto the unit, I had to go home to work for a few hours. If I could have, I would have plugged in my laptop and never left my father's side. I left a message for the doctor and tried to concentrate and get some work done, but wasn't really successful and went back to see my father around dinner time. I brought my fourteen-year-old son with me. I knew seeing his grandfather in a psych ward might upset him, but I was willing to do that if his presence would cheer up my father.

The doctor returned my call while we were visiting. "Your father cannot be released in this condition," he told me.

"So what are you doing for him? He's not even dressed. He hasn't had any exercise all day. What's the plan?"

The doctor told me my father needed time.

"Time won't help," I said. "He is experiencing delirium from his hospital stay and it's only going to get worse the longer he stays there."

"There is no such thing as hospital delirium," he said. Then he told me that the assisted living facility wouldn't take him back because he had been violent and that I either needed to find a skilled nursing facility that would take him or leave him in the hospital until he improved.

I had my marching orders. That night I researched skilled nursing facilities and then I stayed up until 2 a.m. searching the Internet for articles about hospital delirium. No such thing?! It most certainly was a thing, and I started to build a file of proof—although I had no idea what I would use it for. I just knew I had to get my father out of that place.

The next day I toured five nursing homes. I was supposed to be working so I brought my laptop with me, occasionally joining client calls and editing documents from the side of the road. Over the past few years I had perfected my skill of propping the computer up on the steering wheel so I could participate in web calls. The camera angle had to be just right so as to not reveal that I was in a car—and of course still flatter my weak chin.

Sometimes I pulled over just to cry. I couldn't bear the thought of putting my dad in any of the places I saw. They embodied everything I had feared: patients in wheelchairs sitting in halls doing nothing, faint smells of urine lingering in the air. In one of the places I visited the smell was absolutely overpowering. I also noticed that a side door by the patients' rooms was unlocked. I didn't even bother to explain myself to the executive director who was giving me a tour; I just turned and walked out. The place was dirty and unsafe and I had no time for niceties; it was off my list.

IF YOU CAN'T WORK A CALL BUTTON

One facility seemed okay, though. Appearance-wise it was tough and it was located in a neighborhood I wouldn't want to be in late at night. But the staff seemed pleasant; they made eye contact and said hello. At most places I visited, the employees seemed to shuffle around with scowls on their faces and absolutely no energy.

The director there seemed great too. He really listened and I felt like he understood how much I loved my father and how much I wanted him to be well cared for. He said he could accept him despite his violent outburst and that he would go to the hospital the next day to do an intake meeting. I was so relieved.

The appointment was scheduled for 10 a.m. and I expected Cody would call me at 11:00 to update me. But no. I left him a message at 11:01 and heard back from him some time after noon.

"Your father had a good night but unfortunately during his meeting with the nursing home director he said that if he had a machine gun he would shoot all of us. They are not going to take him."

"Oh for god's sake! He can't operate a hospital call button right now. Do you really think he could operate a machine gun?"

I called the man from the nursing home. "My father is not violent. He has dementia. I don't think he's ever even thrown a punch."

"We can't take him. We've already filled the vacancy anyway."

I started sobbing.

"You really need to calm down," he said.

I was furious. This man wasn't sympathetic. Did he think I could stop crying? That I could control myself? He hadn't cared about me or my father at all; he was just looking to fill a bed.

I needed help. I called my cousin the social worker. I was sobbing again before she even said hello. "My father said he was scared!"

She referred me to her friend who worked for a local Council on Aging, who she said might have some nursing home recommendations. She said that I should also call the woman's husband, a lawyer. Ultimately the friend referred me to a nursing home whose executive director said they could handle my father and would treat him for his dementia, not for mental illness or violence. I told them to go ahead and start the intake process. I would tour the facility and figure out how the hell I was going to pay for it later. About a week later, my father moved in.

I lucked out with the nursing home. But caregivers shouldn't have to rely on luck! The eldercare system is broken. Caregivers are left to navigate unfriendly, unhelpful, and overwhelming medical systems on their own. Nursing homes are losing money but still cost too much. Care workers are poorly paid and often overworked. And despite the fact there are approximately five million people currently living with age-related dementia, the disease is sadly misunderstood.

IT'S TIME TO DISRUPT CAREGIVING

In Silicon Valley, tech investors and startup CEOs talk a lot about disruptive innovation, the idea of displacing existing products and industries with new, more efficient inventions and business solutions. Netflix, for example, disrupted television.[1] If ever there was an industry ripe for disruption, it's elder-care.

I was not willing to accept what was considered the norm at that psych ward. I was certainly not going to follow doctor's orders when I knew they were wrong for my father. And I sure as hell wasn't going to leave my Dad under that doctor's so-called care any longer than I was forced to. I had to disrupt the process. Of course, in doing so, my family and work were also disrupted—and not in the good, innovative way. But given the circumstances, I felt that was my best course of action at the time.

Sometimes you will need to disrupt the system on your own in order to access the best care for your parents. The best way to do that is to trust your own knowledge and experience and ensure that you are heard. It means learning to advocate like a boss.

Here are five ways to become a strong advocate for your parents.

1. Play the role.

You are a key member of your parents' care team and you know them best. Do not let anyone relegate you to bystander status. You should expect to be heard. Your observations and opinions are as valid as any professional opinion. That said, you also need to listen. Be open to what doctors, nurses, and other care professionals have to say. Google is a great way to find information on a medical diagnosis or a treatment plan, but it does not give you an MD. And while you do not need to worry about whether or not your parents' medical team likes you (this is no time to be a "good girl"), do keep in mind that you are more likely to be listened to if you are smiling instead of screaming. Frame your comments and questions so that they are about you and your parent and don't put others on the defense. For example, you might say, "Help me understand why my father can't sit on the patio at night," or "What can I do to make sure my mother's meals are low sodium?" or, "If this was your parent, what would you do? I need some advice." Don't be afraid to insist your parents get the best possible care, but do be sure to treat people with respect along the way.

2. Assume good intent.

Be open to the possibility that the care professionals you encounter along your caregiving journey want to help your parents and you. Assume they have good intent. Know that they too are working in an imperfect system, fighting bureaucracy, and navigating insurance companies, so work with them, not against them. Sure, you might meet some bad apples along the way, but don't assume the whole bunch is rotten. Even the doctor in charge of the psych ward had good intent, and in hindsight I can appreciate that. He didn't want to keep my father locked up for some nefarious reason. His role was to stabilize patients. But as my father's advocate, I knew that keeping him in that ward was only going to worsen his symptoms, and so I fought to get him out as soon as possible. I didn't like that the doctor wouldn't release him until certain conditions were met, but I understood it.

3. Humanize your parents.

One of your key functions as a caregiving daughter is to make sure that the people caring for your parents see them as people, not just as patients. Introduce yourself to the nurse assigned to your mother by saying something like, "Hi. I am her daughter and I adore this woman you are taking care of." When I had to ask for a third time to have my father cleaned up and dressed at the psych ward, I said to the nurse, "That man in there is my father. He's someone's grandfather. And we love him. He is not just an old guy with dementia. Please understand that."

4. Be prepared.

Remember that care professionals are busy. Write down questions before you meet with them. Take notes and refer back to them as needed. Bring copies of proxy forms and medication lists and lab results with you to meetings. Respect people's time. If you're going to do research, know that some Internet research is good and some hurts more than it helps. Stick to credible sites like the American Heart Association, the National Cancer Institute, the American Cancer Society, and the Alzheimer's Association. Better yet, ask your parents' doctor or nurse where you can get more information. Use your research to formulate questions, not as gospel.

5. Know your rights.

You know that folder that usually sits on a table in your parents' hospital rooms? Save it. It typically includes a patient bill of rights explaining hospital policies like accessing medical records, refusing care, respecting patient privacy, paying billing, using interpreters, and receiving visitors. It may also provide the name and number of a patient advocate or hospital ombudsman to whom you can direct your concerns. Your parents' primary care doctors most likely also have published patient rights, and insurance companies do too. Likewise, keep a copy of the contracts from the senior living facility. You're not expected to memorize these documents or even read them if you don't encounter an issue. Just know that they exist in the event you do need to reference them. Caregivers also have rights, specifically related to the hospital discharge process. Many states have adopted the Caregiver Advise, Record, and Enable (CARE) Act,[2] which recognizes the critical role family members play as part of the healthcare system and as part of a patient's treatment. Under the CARE Act, family caregivers are supposed to receive an explanation and live instruction of any medical tasks that they will need to perform at home, as well as access to patients' records and timely notification of a patient's release. When you know your rights, you will be more comfortable asserting yourself as your parents' advocate.

PREPARE FOR THE WORST
AND HOPE FOR THE BEST

By developing and using your advocacy skills, you can disrupt a situation that doesn't feel right, a care plan that isn't working, a treatment that seems unnecessary, or a visiting nurse who constantly shows up late. You can also use your advocacy skills to make sure a good situation stays that way.

Yes, the nursing home I moved my father into was a good one, but it wasn't perfect. So I used the caregiver advocacy skills I had honed over the years to make sure he had the best experience he could. I met with the head of the memory care unit to be sure I clearly understood her philosophy and approach to caring for dementia patients. Most importantly, I wanted to be sure I could keep my father out of the hospital. The director was on board. "If he breaks a hip and is in pain, I will call an ambulance," she told me. "Otherwise, I agree there should be no need to hospitalize him." Then she had me sign a no hospitalization form for his file. I appreciated the conversation and the paperwork but I also needed to know how she would ensure that our agreement was enforced. She promised me she would tell all of the staff. Years of caregiving had taught me these details mattered and that it was okay to ask about them.

Whenever my parents went to a new treatment or residential facility, I liked to spend as much time there in the first week as I could to help them get situated. I asked the director if I could work from the unit and she said yes. So I turned the night table in my father's room into a makeshift desk and I held all of my web and phone calls in the residents' library. I wasn't fully productive when I was on site, but I got enough work done that my long-distance coworkers didn't suspect I was handling a family issue—again. And what I didn't get done during the day, I finished at night after my kids went to bed. And once again, I was so grateful for the flexibility I had to work mostly when and where I needed to.

While I was there I made it a point to meet everyone involved in my father's care. I learned the names of the nurses, the aides, the physical therapist, the receptionist, the custodians, and the kitchen staff. I went to the group activities, ate dinner in the dining room, even worked on a jigsaw puzzle with some of the other residents, and I learned my way around the building and the grounds. By investing that time, I knew I could trust the staff, and I earned their trust too. Sometimes, after my father fell asleep, I stuck around to chat with Bob, the night nurse. He was a working son, juggling his job at the nursing home with caring for his elderly parents.

I DON'T KNOW HOW TO HANDLE THIS

About two months after my father had moved in, Bob called me. I was at home, prepping for a business trip.

"Liz, I just sent your father by ambulance to the hospital."

"Are you kidding me? What the hell?"

"He attacked an aide. I'm sorry. I couldn't control him."

Once again, I rushed to the ER. This time, my father was in a locked area designed to keep violent patients from the general population. One of the nurses let me in. My Dad was lying on a gurney in the hallway. He looked so old and frail.

"Hi kid. How'd you know I was here?" He greeted me with a smile. He clearly had no memory of the incident with the aide just an hour earlier.

I asked the admitting nurse what was going to happen and she told me my father would be admitted into the psych ward. The police report said he was a danger to others. He had been "sectioned," involuntarily committed for seventy-two hours.

In the morning I was supposed to fly to California. My company had paid $3,500 dollars to send me to a conference that I had asked to attend, but there was no way I was getting on that plane. This was the second time in months that I had booked work travel and wouldn't go. And while I was worried that not going wouldn't bode well for me—I was missing an industry networking event, and I was costing the firm money—I was not leaving my father. Once again, if I could have quit, I would have. Yes, I needed the money and yes, I had career goals, but this balancing act sucked.

I sent a text to my boss. *My father is in the ER again. I cannot fly to California tomorrow. I don't know how to do this.*

Right after I sent the text, the door to the locked area opened and a man in his twenties was brought in by two police officers. He was handcuffed. I heard the officers telling the admitting nurse that he had been apprehended while brandishing a machete in the street. A machete!

As the officers were leaving, the man thanked them. "Dudes. Thanks. I'm sorry for the trouble. I'm just so messed up. I need help. I know that."

"You gonna behave?" one of them asked.

"I will. I need help."

"Okay. Good luck buddy."

The officer uncuffed him and the nurse brought him into a private room with a cot and a television. I was struck by how this knife-wielding punk was receiving better treatment than my ninety-year old father with dementia.

Crash! About ten minutes after the policemen left, I heard a loud noise from the man's room. Apparently, he had knocked the television to the ground. The nurse called for an attendant to sit outside his door. Crash! I don't know what he knocked over this time.

"Let me out!" he yelled, and he came out of the room and went running for the doors. They were locked so he just banged up against them.

The attendant told him to calm down, but he ran down the hall to the other set of doors, right next to my where my father was lying on his gurney, now asleep. They were also locked.

"There's an elderly gentleman sleeping. Show some respect," the attendant said.

"I don't give a fuck about him and I don't give a fuck about her!" He was now standing in front of me, pointing in my face. My legs started trembling. He stomped back into his room, knocking a medical cart over on his way.

"You need to get out," the attendant said to me and he pointed to the far doors.

"What about my father?" I asked.

"He has to stay in here."

"I am not leaving without him." I tried to sound brave and defiant, hoping my shaking legs wouldn't give me away.

"Fine," he said, grabbed the gurney, ran to the door, and released the lock.

Once my father and I were situated safely against a wall in the main section of the ER, I checked to see if my boss had answered my text.

Who can go in your place?

Seriously? I felt equal parts infuriated, defeated, and exhausted. I had told my boss I was in the emergency room. I did not pretend to be okay. I did not offer to handle the situation. Instead I had expressed vulnerability. *I don't know how to do this.* It was now 11 o'clock at night on the East Coast—only 8 o'clock on the West Coast. Why couldn't she take it from here, I thought? Did she really think I cared about the conference right now? I didn't. I was mildly concerned about how my cancellation would be perceived by my boss and peers, but I would worry about that tomorrow or next week. I had bigger concerns at that moment.

But because I didn't have the energy to say any of that to her, nor did I think that would be too wise, I responded with the names of two people I thought could benefit from the conference and have the flexibility to travel with little notice.

She replied. *Can you reach out to them?*

I wanted to cry. Luckily, I received another text. It was one of my co-workers, also a member of the management team. *I just heard about your father. How can I help you arrange for someone to go to the conference in your place?*

I wrote back. *Honestly, I can't handle this.*

Don't worry about a thing, she replied. *I've got it. Take care of your father.* This woman had taken a leave the year before to be with her mother as she was dying from Alzheimer's. A former working daughter understood and had my back.

We can't expect our bosses or coworkers to read our minds, or even to understand where we are coming from if they have not walked in our shoes. And even if they have, we can't expect them to care about what's happening in our personal lives. That's not their role. We might desperately want them to understand, as I did that night, but that falls under the realm of magical thinking, and as I've said before, magical thinking is a working daughter's enemy. We might think they should because it's good business to give employees the space they need to do deal with life from time to time, especially during times of crisis. But there are no shoulds. And so sometimes disrupting as a caregiver means educating our workplaces about what we need in order to balance our jobs and our eldercare responsibilities.

If you have a caregiving emergency and you just can't or don't want to deal with work, that's your choice. But be clear about it. *My father is in the ER. I cannot travel. I will check in tomorrow and update you on status. Thanks for understanding.* Then be prepared that there may be fallout because you didn't get on the plane and you didn't help recoup the cost of the conference.

But if you do have the headspace and the time to try to minimize the impact of your canceling the trip, offer a solution in your initial outreach. *I'm sorry but I have a family emergency. I am unable to go to the conference tomorrow. I suggest you ask Lynette or Catherine to go. Let me know what you decide and in the morning I can change the hotel reservation to their name. I will also email the conference organizers and let them know who will attend in my place. I will be offline until 9 am ET tomorrow so I can deal with this situation. Thank you for understanding.*

CAREGIVERS ARE GOOD FOR THE ECONOMY

The pressures caregivers feel trying to hang onto their jobs while caregiving, trying to show up for a paid shift after working all night on an unpaid shift, trying to look like they care about work at times when they really don't, and trying to advance a career amid mounting family responsibilities are actually global pressures. The world needs women in the workplace. If women participated in the global economy on an equal basis with men, it would add $28 trillion to the annual global gross domestic product (GDP) by 2025.[3] The

GDP is the monetary value of all the goods and services produced within a specific time period and it is used as an indicator of economic health. Most economists believe that if the GDP is rising, the economy is getting stronger.

The United States is hardly the model for how to treat working mothers. But at least there is a national dialogue about the need for policies that help parents remain in the workforce. And that dialogue brings awareness to the need for change. Elder caregivers are still woefully underrepresented in the conversation. Affordable eldercare has to be part of the conversation when we talk about affordable childcare. Backup eldercare needs to be part of the conversation. Maybe it's time for businesses to instate eldercare leave policies if the federal government won't. It might sound like a wacky idea, but so did the idea of paternity leave at one point. After all, the majority of Americans think caring for two elderly adults would be more difficult than caring for two toddlers.

I am not suggesting that working daughters take on a national advocacy program to change the system. That would be nice, and we would be a force to reckon with, but I know that working daughters are already overloaded with their caregiving responsibilities. What I am suggesting is that we do what we can to disrupt the system in an effort to make balancing eldercare and career more manageable.

Here are four ways to support disrupting the system in support of cultural and legislative change.

1. Start an elder caregiver group at work.

Members of a caregiver support group can brainstorm solutions to real-life struggles, act as a support network for each other, and alleviate some of the loneliness that comes with eldercare. Jot down your vision for a support group at work. Who is your target audience? How often will you meet? Where will you meet? Talk to human resources about your idea and ask for support in getting the group started. If you don't have an HR department, take your concept to your boss.

2. Change the conversation.

When you encounter a conversation about the need to support parents in the workplace, mention the need to also support workers with parents too. If you read an article or blog post, you can participate via the comments section. Simply remind people:

    a. that there are forty-four million unpaid family caregivers in the United States and the majority of them also work for pay;[4]

b. that we live in a rapidly aging society and experts predict we will have a shortage of paid caregivers in just a few years;

c. that women are having fewer children on average—1.77 births per women, down 3.8 percent since 2015, leaving fewer daughters to do the caring;[5]

d. that the unpaid work caregivers do makes all other work possible and fills gaps in the broken system that does not adequately provide for our senior citizens;

e. that caregivers, and the elderly they are caring for, deserve better;

f. and that eldercare must be part of the conversation about workplace reform.

3. Support organizations that support caregivers.

Paid caregivers, the ones we rely on to care for our parents so that we can go to work, are mostly women. Many of them are women of color and immigrant women and are often underpaid.[6] These domestic workers are often not protected by the Fair Labor Standards Act and therefore not required to receive minimum wage, healthcare benefits, or paid sick days.[7] An organization called the National Domestic Workers Alliance (NDWA) is trying to improve the working conditions of all domestic workers, including eldercare workers. Visit its website (https://www.domesticworkers.org) to learn more, call your state legislators in support of the policies NDWA is trying to pass, and amplify the organization's work on your social media channels by sharing their posts. Disrupting this industry has to include valuing the work of both paid and unpaid caregivers.

4. Vote.

Make your voice heard at the polls. AARP regularly publishes updates on legislation, by state, that has an impact on eldercare on its website (www. AARP.org). Find out where candidates stand on issues like caregiver tax credits, the Social Security personal needs allowance, which sets the amount of money people in nursing homes can keep for personal items, Medicare reform, and retirement savings plans. Then cast a vote in support of care.

REPEAT AFTER ME

But perhaps the most important disrupting you can do as a working daughter is to disrupt your own thought processes to try and stop the cycle of guilt because you feel like you should be doing more. You are one person. You are playing a team sport but you are the only player on the field. You are doing the best you can. And you know what? Your best is pretty damn incredible.

To help you acknowledge that you are doing a damn good job at this caregiving thing, find a mantra and put it on auto play in your head. As I mentioned, my mantra for tough times is "The only way through is through." Say your mantra over and over until you truly believe it.

Here are six mantras to inspire you.

1. It's okay. This is how it's supposed to be.

A fellow working daughter shared this concept with me. No matter what happens, tell yourself this is how it is supposed to be.

2. I am enough.

Yes, yes you are.

3. Do your best and screw the rest.

This one also came from a fellow working daughter. And it's perfect. What else can you do?

4. Breathe. Everything else is optional.

Think about it; it's true.

5. I am a force for good.

Damn straight! You are a gift!

6. Life is tough. But I'm tougher.

Tougher than you realize. Trust me.

The fact of the matter is this: caregiving *will* disrupt your life unless we disrupt caregiving and the existing work culture together first!

Chapter Eight

Renew

"You need to take care of yourself." On a Friday afternoon, less than a week after I had rushed to my parents' house following the alarming call from my sister telling me something was wrong with my parents, I called my boss to give her an update. I was sitting in a wheelchair in the lobby of Quincy Hospital; it was the quietest spot I could find even though the sliding doors to the parking lot kept opening and shutting and ambulance sirens wailed incessantly. Because she was in California and I was in Boston, she wasn't aware that I was in full-on crisis mode, that I had barely logged fourteen hours of work that week, much less forty, and that I was hanging on by a thread. That's when she told me to take care of myself.

Could there be any more well-intentioned but frustrating words for a caregiver to hear? As someone responsible for the well-being of others, caregivers are acutely aware of the need to stay healthy and strong. After all, if something happens to you, who is going to take on your responsibilities? Who will care for you? How are you going to recover if you can't take time to rest and recuperate? Breadwinning caregivers feel an extra pressure—you must stay strong not only for the people you care for but also so you can continue to provide for your family. And you certainly can't afford to take sick time, if you even have it, not when you're using it all up to take your children and your parents to the doctor.

"I know I need to take care of myself," I said. "What I don't know is how." I was operating on four hours of sleep, two bags of Twizzlers, two coffees, and three Diet Cokes that day. I knew eight hours of REM sleep and a bag of kale would have been better, but how the hell was I supposed to make that happen? I was about to leave the hospital where my father was being treated and drive back to the Cape in summer Friday traffic to pack my mother's stuff and move her into an assisted living facility. Sleep and salad were not in my future.

"I know it's easier said than done," my boss said. "Can you pick one thing to do? Are you drinking enough water?"

I couldn't remember my last glass. "I'll hydrate," I said.

"Good," she said. "Hydration is key."

Two days later, when I returned to my own home, I grabbed my Camelbak water bottle and committed to drinking three liters of water a day. I still skimped on sleep; I needed as many hours awake as possible to be with my parents and deal with work, doctors, lawyers, estate planning, and insurance. I still subsisted mostly on Diet Coke and Twizzlers; chewing on the strawberry vines helped me relax. At night, no matter how late I got home, I poured myself a big glass of Sauvignon Blanc as both a way to treat myself and to counter all of the caffeine in my system. And if the Twizzlers hadn't filled me that day, I would eat a sleeve of Oreos with the wine. I was hardly a model for self-care, but at least I wasn't dehydrated.

I was, however, exhausted and suffering from nightmares. One night, after I had decided to transfer my mother to an assisted living facility near me (and, as a result, lost the deposit at the respite facility on the Cape where she had originally been staying), I dreamed that her primary care physician told me I had made a mistake and that I should move her again. The dream spiraled from there. In one scene I lay face down in a pile of mulch, sobbing. In another, I was topless in a New York City park. If I had been in therapy (I wanted—and needed—to be, but my copay was high and I was worried about money), I'm sure a doctor could have spent hours interpreting the dream's meaning. Another night, after a particularly annoying trip to the grocery store to buy Depends—the store had been full of retirees and I felt like there was no escape from the elderly—I dreamed I was being chased by tracker jackers, the genetically engineered wasps that attack humans in the dystopian science fiction trilogy *The Hunger Games*. And right after I moved my mother into a hospice house, I dreamed I cut off all of my hair and died.

And to make matters worse, I looked like hell too. I walked around all summer with a chipped front tooth. Stress had caused me to grind my teeth so hard that I cracked one in late June and I had no time to get it repaired. When I had to go to New York for a client meeting, it felt like an effort just to apply eyeliner and mascara. I put my hair in a bun that I hoped came across more like a chignon, and I tried not to smile or open my mouth too much in hopes that no one would notice my tooth.

Sometimes when I sat in doctors' waiting rooms with one of my parents, I looked around at the other daughters accompanying their elderly parents. These women were middle aged and frumpy, and I wondered how they could let themselves go. Then I'd catch a glimpse of myself in a window or a mirror and realize I looked just like them—putting on weight, wearing sweats and no makeup, my wet hair pulled back in a ponytail, my gray roots in need of a dye job, my broken tooth.

"You know what one of my biggest fears is?" I said to my sister. "That I'll completely give up and start carrying a Vera Bradley bag." Those quilted, floral, cotton handbags are the opposite of style in my opinion. But the waiting rooms were full of them. So was the assisted living place.

"See?" I would say to my sister when I spotted another tired, middle-aged caregiver carrying one. "I'm a heartbeat away from Vera."

"You're crazy," she'd respond, and we'd laugh.

I couldn't stop my mother's cancer from spreading. I couldn't stop my father's dementia from progressing. But if I could just hang on, I could control what purse I carried—and it would never be quilted or sold next to greeting cards.

On Sunday, August 3, I wrote in my diary, "Double Stuff and wine are getting boring," and I noted that my daughter had climbed in my lap that night and counted the wrinkles on my forehead. You know those comparison photos of two-term U.S. presidents when they enter the White House and when they leave? They take office looking young and vital and they exit eight years later looking like they served for sixteen? I think I aged that much that weekend.

It had been an especially brutal few days. Just two weeks after we moved my mother into assisted living, we had to move her out and into a hospice home. I had hoped she could live the rest of her months enjoying life in senior housing, meeting new friends and being cared for. Only a few days before she went to the hospice home, she told me she noticed there were strings of lights in the trees outside her apartment window and she couldn't wait to see the place decorated for Christmas. But she would never see the lights; she wouldn't live to Christmas. Instead she would spend her final months in a small room, tethered to an oxygen tank, surrounded by dying people.

But through it all, I stayed hydrated.

I drank water for several reasons. First, I had made a promise to my boss and I simply wanted to keep my word. Second, because I wasn't carrying my fair share of the work and responsibility at the office, the least I could do was try to take care of myself so that when I did contribute, it would make an impact. I had read that self-care made people more successful at work.[1] And finally, I knew that doing something for myself, no matter how minor, made me feel like I was in control of at least one tiny part of my life—in addition to my choice of purse.

As the weeks progressed, I started to do more things for myself. I took walks around my neighborhood and short jogs around the track near the hospice. Before client meetings, I squeezed in a manicure just so I could feel somewhat pulled together. I had my tooth repaired, albeit nine weeks after it chipped. It wasn't that the crisis was easing up, because it was not. It was that my attitude had changed.

When my parents first got sick, I thought I would just power through until things got back to normal. As the weeks went on, I realized this was my new normal, and I had to find a way to live in that new reality. I found that taking care of myself, even in the tiniest ways, gave me a sense of control that I clearly needed.

One night, toward the end of my mother's life, I was sitting by her bed. She was sleeping more than she was awake at that point. When she woke up, she took my hand and said, "I worry about you the most."

"Me?" I said, "I'm the competent one."

My life was falling apart but my ego was clearly intact. Surely she knew I had handled most of the logistics during this crisis. She fell back asleep and I sat there wondering why me?

Months after she died, I was struggling. I thought my responsibilities would ease up after her death but, as I told my husband, I felt just as stressed as I did when the caregiving crisis first struck. The insurance companies were so difficult to deal with—they wanted me to fill out piles of paperwork, they kept me on hold when I was at work, and they were slow to pay out policies that I needed to cover my Dad's rent. There were so many doctors' appointments to reschedule for my father, appointments I didn't have time to make while my mother was still alive. I felt like a failure at work, still so behind on my goals from all of the time I had missed. And my aunt passed away, leaving me with a condo to clean out. Plus I was finally starting to grieve. And one day, as I felt my knees start to buckle under me again, I realized why my mother had been worried about me: it was because I would always be responsible for this family.

One universal truth of caregiving is, "There's always one." There is always one sibling or family member who manages the bulk of the caregiving duties. It's usually a daughter, and while many people think it would fall to the adult child with the least complicated life—the one with no children or the least stressful job, for example—that's not the case. My mother's hospice nurse Peg once told me she looked for three things in a caregiver: devotion, brains and competence. If you possess those qualities, you most likely have a pretty full life. And regardless of your other commitments, you are most likely "the one." My mother recognized that in our family I am the one. Her concern, it turns out, was warranted and also a compliment.

When I accepted the fact that my caregiver role wasn't ending, it was merely changing, I went looking for the suitcase we packed up from my mother's hospice room the night she died. For months it had remained in the trunk of my car unopened. I was hoping I'd find a small, red silk butterfly inside of it. I had picked up the butterfly in the parking lot of Quincy Hospital that day when I called my boss. My mother loved butterflies and so I had taped it to the television set in her hospice room. When I found it tucked in the pocket of the suitcase, I taped it to the mirror over my bureau so I too could look at it every day and draw strength from it. I took a sip of water and once again accepted my new normal. I could do this.

Sometimes caregiving sneaks up on you and you live in that role for years. Sometimes it hits you hard and fast, starting and ending in a whirlwind. No matter the circumstances, you do need to take care of yourself to the best of your ability, if for no other reason than you won't be able to help others if you're not okay yourself. And when you do meet your own needs, you are better able to realize the caregiver's gain, the physical and mental strength that can come from taking care of someone else.

THE TWO MOST COMMON LIMITING BELIEFS OF CAREGIVERS

Finding time for self-care can be difficult. I get it; you're busy. So am I. Women, especially the devoted, smart, competent ones, handle, on average, more housework and childcare than men do. They typically manage the so-called invisible tasks too. But sometimes it's not just time getting in the way of your ability to care for yourself. Sometimes it's your own limiting beliefs, thoughts that constrain you in some way. These beliefs can be based on your religious views, the way you were raised, your personality types, or your lifelong habits. Here are two of those most common limiting beliefs of caregivers as well as strategies to move past them.

1. No one else can do what I do/as well as I do it.

This might actually be a true statement. Perhaps no one else can do what you're doing as well as you're doing it. Or maybe you're worried that your parents only want you to help them. Well you know what? Sometimes we need to accept good enough. I know it's hard to deny the people we are caring for what they want. I know it can be uncomfortable to say no. But when those requests are causing you undue stress, you don't have to deliver—especially if you can offer a comparable alternative. A job completed is still a job completed.

Make a list of the tasks you do as a caregiver and then identify a few that don't require perfection. Maybe you're not ready to give up attending doctors' appointments because you want to make sure you get all of your questions answered, or you don't feel comfortable asking anyone else to help with money management and bill paying. But are you really the only one who can clean the house? Does it really matter if someone else buys the groceries and brings home the wrong brand of paper towels? It does not. Let it go.

This type of limiting belief is often rooted in martyr syndrome. I recognize it because I'm pretty good at it. In order to move past martyrdom, ask yourself, "What am I gaining from taking on all of the burden?" Do you like getting sympathy from others? Are you uncomfortable sharing the spotlight? Does your caregiver role make you feel special? Do you think you don't deserve joy without suffering? Be honest with yourself about why you are taking on as much as you are. I'd be lying if I didn't admit that I get an ego boost from being "the one."

It's important to understand the feelings that are driving your actions. Expecting external rewards for your choices will leave you frustrated and often disappointed. Reward yourself instead. Acknowledge your contributions by treating yourself to some type of self-care. When you shift from wanting others to acknowledge and reward you, you shift from feeling like a victim to feeling like someone who is in control. You shift from feeling the burden to experiencing the gain.

2. Thinking of myself at a time like this would be selfish.

No, it would not. If others are truly dependent on you for their well-being, then isn't it selfish to leave your well-being to chance? The best way to combat limiting beliefs is to change your perception. Historically, women have been seen as people who provide care, not people who prioritize their own needs. If you have internalized that belief then consider this: caring for yourself is not taking time away from caregiving; it is part of caregiving. It is part of what you must do to effectively care for someone else. As the feminist poet Audra Lorde wrote, "Caring for myself is not self-indulgence, it is self-preservation, and that is an act of political warfare."[2] Is it selfish to stop and put gas in your car when the tank is low? No, it's necessary in order to keep driving.

And refueling doesn't just mean taking care of your physical needs, like eating something other than Twizzlers or getting a decent night's sleep. Even if you choose to get a pedicure or hit a bucket of golf balls instead of spending an extra half hour visiting your parents or cleaning out your email inbox, you should do so unapologetically. Whatever destresses you and feeds your soul is good for everyone involved. Trust me, I know from personal experience; a bitter caregiver can do more harm than good.

Of course, sometimes this belief is steeped in something a bit more complicated. Sometimes caregivers struggle with saying no, especially the women. If that's true for you, say yes instead. Think of the three to five most important things you need to do as a caregiver—taking care of yourself is one of them. Anytime anything comes up that might interfere with you doing those three to five things—requests from other people, additional caregiving tasks that could be delegated to someone else, attending an optional brainstorming session at the office—don't say no. Instead say yes to your most important tasks. Say yes to the hour at the gym that you've decided is critical for your well-being. If the request interferes with your workout, your "no" becomes easy. I call it getting to no through yes.

FIFTY THINGS CAREGIVERS CAN DO TO PRACTICE SELF-CARE

Here are fifty different ways caregivers can practice self-care. Most of them are simple, a few require more effort. I want you to pick one thing from this list, no matter how small, and commit to doing it for a week. If you don't like it, try something else the next week. If it works for you, keep at it. As you find your strength and settle in to each new phase of your caregiving—your "new normal"—add more things.

1. Drink water.

As my boss said to me at the beginning of my caregiving crisis, "hydration is key." Drinking water is the simplest thing you can do to take care of yourself. And it packs a huge punch. By helping blood to transport oxygen and other nutrients to your cells, water increases your energy levels.[3] What caregiver doesn't need that? Water also helps build strong muscles, which many caregivers need to assist with bathing and helping family members in and out of chairs and beds. The National Academy of Sciences Food and Nutrition Board says women should try to drink 91 ounces of water per day and men should try for 125 ounces,[4] so keep a water bottle with you at all times.

2. Take walks.

Research shows that taking a walk during the day increases a person's enthusiasm for his or her job, reduces nervousness, and improves relaxation.[5] Whether you get paid or not, caregiving is a job. And walking for thirty minutes five times a week can also improve blood pressure, decrease risk of heart disease, improve joint pain, and lower your blood sugar.[6]

3. Sweat.

According to the Mayo Clinic, "virtually any form of exercise . . . can act as a stress reliever."[7] Exercise improves your mood, lowering symptoms associated with mild depression and anxiety. It improves your sleep, and of course it improves your physical health. If you're not much of an exerciser or it's been a while since you last worked out, try a program like Couch to 5K. It eases you into exercising but still delivers the benefits.

4. Nap.

Naps are a great way to reenergize during the day. A fifteen- to twenty-minute nap will make you feel more alert. Sleep expert Sara C. Mednick, PhD, says a longer nap can help with decision making, a critical skill for caregivers.[8] Naps are also a great way to make up for nighttime sleep deficits. If, like many caregivers, you suffer from insomnia, this is key. When I worked in an office, I used to book one of the conference rooms every afternoon. I'd lock the door, draw the blinds, set the timer on my iPhone for twenty minutes, lie down on the floor, and recharge.

5. Keep in touch with your friends.

"I have no time for friends," you're thinking. Neither did I in the midst of my caregiving crisis, but I found texting to be a really effective way to stay connected. Sometimes I didn't want to have a voice conversation; I wasn't in the mood to talk, or I was sitting next to my mother while she was sleeping, but I appreciated hearing from my friends and cousins via text. It made me feel supported, gave me the chance to ask about their lives, and reminded me there were other things going on in the world that were unrelated to me or my parents.

6. Bring your friends to you.

In my mother's last weeks, I wanted to spend every spare moment I had with her and well-meaning friends wanted to spend time with me. They rightfully thought I could use a break and some fun time. I decided, rather than pushing them off, I would take them up on their offers to get together and have dinner, but on terms that worked for me. I met friends for dinner at a restaurant near the hospice house, so I could be with my mother before I went out and again after. And my cousins joined my sister and me for takeout in the living room of the hospice house so we could get a decent meal, share memories and laugh, and know that if our mother needed us, we were just a flight of stairs away.

7. Get a manicure.

When you feel like your whole world is falling apart, you're wearing the same three outfits day after day, and your hair is wet, unkempt, and pulled back, a manicure can give you a boost. When your hands are polished, you feel more polished. And anything you can do to feel more in control helps. I squeezed manicures in by asking the manicurist to simply cut, push, and file. By going for the "mini" manicure, I was able to cut a forty-minute salon visit down to twenty minutes, and that made me feel less stressed about making the time for me.

8. Read a book.

Reading a book can give you a break from your own thoughts. During the summer and fall when my parents were sick, I read a book about a psych ward and two books about cancer. Despite the heavy topics and how close to home they hit, I appreciated hearing someone else's story and taking a break from thinking about my own. I also read some David Sedaris, who made me laugh out loud. Serious or funny, give your own thoughts a break and escape into someone else's by reading.

9. Binge watch television.

Seriously. It helps to have something (aside from—or in addition to—a glass of wine) to look forward to at the end of a long day of caregiving. Even bad television does the trick. The idea is to escape reality for an hour or two and give yourself a break from your day-to-day challenges. I shocked my sister after one particularly rough week when I told her, "I am going to Port Charles tonight." She wasn't surprised to learn I watched *General Hospital*; she was surprised I admitted it. But sometimes a little Luke Spencer is just what the doctor ordered!

10. Craft.

Caregiving can be a good time to take up knitting or start making jewelry. There is so much waiting involved in caregiving—at someone's bedside, at the doctor's office or hospital, in the pharmacy, on hold. Creating something can reduce your stress level[9] and give you a sense of accomplishment that is often lacking in caregiving.

11. Spend time with children.

There's nothing like youth to counterbalance aging and dying. Play on the floor. Play make believe. Laugh and sing. Just play.

12. Volunteer.

One of the simplest ways to escape from your own troubles and get out of your head is to give back to others. Caregiving is often an isolating, lonely experience. Volunteering creates a connection between you and the people you are helping, other volunteers, and a cause. While signing up to co-chair the elementary school Halloween Dance during my mother's final weeks may have been a bit crazy, it provided a distraction and something to look forward to during a sad and stressful time.

13. Engage in random acts of kindness.

Just days before my mother died, my friend asked people to mark the anniversary of her son's death by performing a random act of kindness for a stranger. It was a small gesture, but it felt so good to buy coffee for the person in the car behind me at the Starbucks drive through on my way to the hospice house that morning.

14. Listen.

When it feels like your world is crashing in on you and that you are the only one going through a hard time, put your own problems aside for a while and listen to a friend share her problems. They might not seem as large as yours, or they might seem larger; it doesn't matter. Everybody needs someone to hear them and it feels good to be that person.

15. Enroll in therapy.

When you're dealing with inordinate amounts of stress and facing illness and end-of-life issues, it is incredibly beneficial to have a professional help you sort out complex feelings around family and dying. If your insurance covers therapy, take advantage of it. Your mental health affects your physical health.

16. Get outside.

Get some fresh air, especially if you're spending most of your days in institutions like hospitals or senior housing. Look at the sky, study the clouds, and let nature heal you. Studies show people who spend time in green spaces have lower stress levels. [10]

17. Keep a journal.

I kept a diary every day of my crisis. Even though I didn't have time to sit down and write every day, I dictated my thoughts to Siri on my iPhone. Recapping what I did and how I felt was not only a way for me to chronicle all that was happening, but it also helped me understand my feelings. According to James Pennebaker, a University of Texas at Austin psychologist and researcher, journaling has a positive impact on physical well-being. [11] It can strengthen your immune system and help you cope with stressful events because it helps you learn from your emotions.

18. Shop online.

When you're in the middle of a stressful time, treat yourself to something fun. When my parents were sick, I bought myself a few necklaces at Bauble-Bar, an inexpensive online jewelry store. Those little baubles helped cheer me up.

19. Have a glass of wine or a cup of tea.

When my parents were both sick, I would look forward to pouring myself a glass of wine every night. Even if I fell asleep before I drank it, which happened many nights, the act of pouring that glass of wine was my way of marking the end of another long day. It wasn't about what was in the glass, pouring it was merely a symbolic act; I had survived another day.

20. Do yoga.

A regular yoga practice helps you relax during the day and sleep at night. [12] Taking a class in a studio can require a significant time commitment, but you can easily practice with an online video or app.

21. Listen to music.

Neuroscientists have proven that listening to music increases the positive emotions people feel. [13] Download the music that moves you to your iPod or smart phone and create a positive soundtrack for your otherwise stressful life.

22. Clean.

When our homes are clean, especially when they are clutter free, we feel more in control of our lives. I am not advocating you add housework to your to-do list—unless you are the kind of person who finds housework relaxing. But if you can try to stay in control of clutter, or you have the luxury of hiring someone to clean up after you, it does wonders for the soul.

23. Buy yourself flowers.

As a caregiver, you're probably running lots of errands, so make one of those errands for you. Pick up a bouquet of flowers for yourself and put them on your kitchen counter or your desk at work. If someone asks who they're from, tell them they're from someone who loves you.

24. Get a massage.

If you can only find one hour in the week to dedicate to your well-being, getting a massage is a great option. According to the Mayo Clinic, massages are an effective treatment for reducing stress, pain, and muscle tension.[14]

25. Breathe.

Practice deep breathing techniques. Breathing exercises have been proven to help fend off the fight or flight response we often feel in stressful situations and help manage our moods by decreasing feelings of anger and anxiety. Inhale through your nose for a count of four and then exhale for a count of four. Most wellness experts suggest doing this for ten minutes a day, but even five minutes will make a difference. Do this every morning to start the day or at night to end it.

26. Meditate.

Studies have shown meditation not only lowers stress levels but can also boost your immune system.[15] For an overworked, overtired, overly stressed caregiver, that can be key. You can learn to meditate through books, websites, and even apps. Headspace and Calm are two apps that guide you through brief, daily meditations.

27. Join a support group.

Our feelings as caregivers are complex. Sometimes we feel like no one understands what we're going through—but other caregivers do. Support groups help you feel less isolated[16] and are often great places to discover new resources to help you. You can join the Working Daughter support group on Facebook or call your local Office of Elder Affairs for a listing of groups near you.

28. Practice gratitude.

Sometimes as caregivers, we forget that we have anything to be happy about. Every morning we wake up to face overwhelming to-do lists, scary medical news, and possible end-of-life moments. But we're waking up and that's something to be happy about! Research shows that taking the time to acknowledge what we are thankful for can help us put difficult situations into perspective, reduce our stress, and make us happier.[17] Set a timer for one to five minutes and list all of the things, big and small, you are grateful for. It might be your own health. It might be a strong cup of coffee. Don't edit your list, just say thank you.

29. Take a bath.

More than making us feel pampered, a quick soak in the tub can also help lower our stress levels, improve our circulation, relax our muscles, and help us sleep better. And if you choose to add bubbles, candles, or essential oils, even better.

30. Spend time with animals.

Type "caregivers and animals" into Google and you'll find lots of articles telling you how animal therapy can help the person you are caring for. But animals can help you too. Pets can make you feel less alone and provide you unconditional love, something you will absolutely crave during your caregiving journey.

31. Bake.

Baking has been found to be therapeutic[18] because it stimulates the senses and can be meditative, so why not try making some cupcakes or cookies to ease your troubles? Whether or not you actually eat what you make is optional.

32. Hit a bucket of golf balls.

Go to the nearest driving range (there are indoor driving ranges you can visit in the winter) and order a bucket of balls. If you're an experienced golfer, you already know how concentrating on your swing can clear your mind. If you're not a golfer, you'll forget all about your real troubles as you struggle to hit the ball. And no matter your skill level, it feels good to whack a ball when you're feeling stressed. Batting cages have the same effect.

33. Ask for and/or accept help.

Admit it: there is too much to do by yourself. But so many people, especially women, automatically reply, "No thank you. I'm all set," when someone offers to help them. If you're like me, you're kicking yourself right after the words come out of your mouth but turning down offers of support is a lifelong habit that is hard to break. To change that, keep in mind that the person offering most likely wants to help you and by refusing you are denying that person the opportunity to feel useful and supportive. (Revisit the process for managing offers of help in chapter 1.)

34. Maintain a morning routine.

Highly successful people swear by their morning routines. Unless you sleep through your alarm and are running late for a meeting, you have the opportunity to control your morning. Spend as much of it as you can how you want and prepare yourself for the day ahead. Exercise. Meditate. Practice gratitude. Create a waking routine. Do whatever it is that makes you feel good about getting out of bed.

35. Eat chocolate.

One of my cousins eats a dark chocolate Hershey Kiss every night after dinner. She loves the taste and says that one Kiss makes her happy. I think she's crazy—how can one tiny piece of chocolate satisfy anyone? But science supports the way she feels. Dark chocolate can boost endorphins in your brain.[19] So go ahead and indulge. As a caregiver, I need all the endorphins I can get. So I eat just one too—one bag, that is!

36. Garden.

When you're a caregiver, you are forced to face end-of-life issues on a regular basis. Counter that by growing something. Whether you plant in containers, on your own property, or in a community garden, this is an activity that is good for your soul. And research out of the Netherlands suggests gardening is a great stress buster.[20]

37. Dine out.

As a caregiver, you are always waiting on someone else. Depending on your schedule and your budget, schedule a regular night out at a restaurant and let someone else wait on you.

38. Avoid social media.

Sure, social media can be a good way to stay connected with friends and family. It can also be a great way to feel lousy about yourself fast. Several studies show that people feel depressed after spending time on Facebook because comparing their lives to the lives of others makes them feel bad.[21] When you're spending the summer visiting the psych ward, what good will come from seeing photos of your friends visiting the beach? Log off and read a book instead!

39. Grab your security blanket.

Security blankets aren't just for toddlers or Linus from Peanuts. The life of a caregiver is full of insecurity. Am I making the right decisions? How long will this last? Can I do this? Find an inanimate object that brings you comfort and keep it with you—a comfy sweater or a soft blanket could even come in handy in an over-air-conditioned hospital room should you find yourself taking the night shift. But anything that makes you feel safe, strong, and good can double as a security blanket: a piece of jewelry, a pebble, a lucky coin—anything!

40. Sing.

When you sing, you send musical vibrations through your body. These vibrations can alter your mood.[22] I had a song that I played in my car every time I turned onto the street where my mother's hospice house was. I would crank up the volume and sing along to the song and prepare myself for whatever I was about to encounter. So on the way to your next appointment, roll up those car windows and belt one out.

41. Read motivational quotes.

Need a boost of support or inspiration to get you through another challenging and long day? Read some motivational quotes to inspire you. You can buy a book of quotes or pin your favorites on Pinterest and look at them every day.

42. Listen to podcasts.

Podcasts are becoming more and more popular and, as a result, there is more and more fantastic content available for you to listen to at your convenience. Choose from great storytelling, motivational interviews, or life hacks that can help you manage your day.

43. Create your own personal rest area.

Whether it's your favorite comfy chair, a bench in the park, the beach, or a booth in your favorite coffee shop, create a "happy place" place where you can go to escape from the day and then visit that place when you need a break.

44. Pray.

There's power in prayer, so if you are religious, make time for prayer every day. Pray where and when you can—in the car, in waiting rooms, and in checkout lines. Prayer doesn't have to be perfect to be powerful.

45. Dance.

Dancing can be a way to relax. It can also be a way to laugh, abandon your troubles, and forget about your day-to-day life. A study out of Sweden showed people suffering from depression who danced weekly experienced a positive boost in their mood.[23] So whether you take a dance class, go out on the town, or just dance in your living room, cut up that rug.

46. Pay someone a compliment.

When you're a caregiver, especially the primary caregiver, sometimes you feel like you're the only one who gets things done. Give yourself some perspective, and a dose of good feelings, by making someone else feel good. During my caregiving crisis, I sent friends candles with the words "You're awesome, just like me" on them. It lifted me up to lift up someone else.

47. Visit a museum.

Art lifts us up, transports us, challenges us, and inspires us. Lose yourself for an hour, an afternoon, or maybe a day in a local art museum. I live close to the world-famous Museum of Fine Arts Boston and the Museum of Bad Art. Visiting either one instantly boosts my mood.

48. Take the day off.

No one can go all day every day. We all need a break. Take a day off and ignore your to-do list. Sure, your list of tasks will be waiting for you when you return, but the down time will be good for you.

49. Floss.

You know you're supposed to see the dentist every six months for a cleaning. But what's the first appointment you cancel when life gets crazy? If you're like many working daughters I know, you justify that an annual cleaning is good enough. And then you miss that appointment.

I get it; I sported a chipped front tooth for months. Whether you make it to your appointment or not, aim to floss every night. The American Dental Association recommends cleaning between your teeth daily in order to prevent plaque and avoid tooth decay and gum disease.[24] Personally, flossing makes me feel like a rock star. "I got the kids to school, took my Dad to the doctor, delivered a kick ass presentation at work, and I flossed. Oh yeah!"

50. Use respite care.

Maybe you need more than a day off. Maybe you need a week's vacation, you're traveling for work, or you have some personal needs that require attention. Consider respite care. Many assisted living facilities offer thirty-day respite stays so you can take time off and know the person you take care of is in good hands.

Let's make a deal. I'll spare you the clichés about oxygen masks and sharpening saws, if you promise to commit to something on this list.

Chapter Nine

Plan

"Please tell me you have a plan and you won't ever put me through this," my niece blurted out to my sister. They were flying home after visiting my parents during that crisis summer of 2014. I don't think my niece was implying she wouldn't be willing to care for her mother someday. I believe she was reacting to how emotionally spent my sister was after a week of helping to move our mother into respite care and sort through our parents' house, throwing away unneeded items and filing important paperwork, visiting our father in the hospital, and coming to terms with the fact that neither parent would likely ever return home.

My daughter, who was eight at the time, was just as direct in discussing my future. We were staying with my parents after my mother took a bad fall and broke her nose during the summer of 2011. She asked me why I was always going into the bathroom with Nana. But before I could answer, her eyes widened. She had figured it out on her own. "Oh . . . you're *helping* her in there?" she asked, to be sure. "If you ever need help when you're old, ask Joe." Apparently, she expected her brother to be a working son someday.

At some point in your caregiving journey, you'll realize you should make some plans related to your own future. Maybe, like my sister and me, your children have told you, "Don't ever put me through what I've watched you go through." Perhaps your firsthand experience as a working daughter trying to care for a parent while holding down a job and raising a family has inspired you to plan for the future so that your own children can have a different caregiving experience. You want to ensure your daughters and sons will be able to pursue their career goals even as you age and perhaps require assistance. So many working daughters have told me, "I vow never to put my own child through this." Perhaps witnessing the stress your parents experience worrying about their health, their homes, and their finances as they get older has motivated you to do whatever you can now to minimize stress in your life later on. Or maybe you don't have children and so you know you need to arrange for future care. No matter your motivation, act now and prepare as best you can.

STUFF MATTERS

I was inspired to take action after spending an afternoon helping my mother sort and shred old bank and insurance statements. When I returned home that day my husband was sitting at the desk in our living room. "We've got to clean out that desk now!" I said. Like most families I know, we have a junk drawer in our kitchen. It's full of random items like keys to who knows where, screwdrivers, tape measures, birthday candles, and flashlights. But we also have a second junk drawer in the living room desk and it's full of receipts, coins, and pens, half of which probably no longer have ink in them. "If we don't clean that desk out now, our kids are going to have to do it someday. We can't do that to them!"

Granted, I'm a little sensitive about other people's stuff. Because I bought the house I grew up in from my parents, and because they didn't clean out the attic or the basement before they moved, I also bought thirty-five years' worth of their stuff. I have two antique stereo consoles with turntables. One is cool in a retro kind of way. Two is excessive. I have three large wooden desks. I have an assortment of chairs and a credenza full of depression glass. I'd like to drag some of the excess furniture to the curb and put a "Free" sign on it, but it's too heavy for one person to move and my husband hates to throw anything away because he believes "we might need it someday."

And as if my parents' hand me downs aren't enough, I've started to "acquire" my mother-in-law's things too. One day after Kevin and I had been living in our house for a few years, I came home from work to find a large maple table with matching chairs in my dining room. The cheap table that I had bought when we were first married, and that I still liked, was pushed against the wall.

"What's this?" I asked my husband.

"It's my mother's. She doesn't want it," he said.

"Neither do I."

"Well it's too nice to throw away and she wanted someone to have it."

"So I'm stuck with it?

"What's wrong with it? It's a really nice table."

"Sure, if you're seventy-five," I said.

When it came time to clean out my parents' house on Cape Cod, I was happy to learn that two thrift shops had opened up within a two-mile radius of my parents' house. But when I went online to see what items the shops accepted, I knew it wasn't going to be easy. No twin beds. No dry sinks. No maple furniture whatsoever. No to pretty much everything I wanted to get rid of. I decided I'd try a yard sale and one Saturday morning that summer, I dragged the dry sink, a tea cart, a wooden rocking chair, the kitchen set, a mauve upholstered wingback chair, some bedroom furniture, and boxes and boxes of knickknacks out on to the front lawn. My aunt, who was staying in the family cottage next door that weekend, was horrified.

"The Hitchcock kitchen set?" she said. "You're not going to sell it are you? Those end tables are Cushman Colonial! That's really good maple. I remember when your mother bought her bedroom set. We were all jealous that she bought Cushman. How much are you selling it for?"

I tried to cover up the price tags I had made with a Sharpie and Post-It notes. I was practically giving things away, and in fact was more than happy to.

My aunt called her daughter over. "Will these fit in your car?" she asked pointing to the night tables. "I'm buying them."

"Thanks a lot," my cousin said to me. She knew that now she would have to unload the Cushman Colonial someday.

It's no wonder that an article on the PBS online magazine *Next Avenue* titled "Sorry, Nobody Wants Your Parents' Stuff"[1] has remained one of the most read and shared items on the site since it was first published more than a year ago. The gist of the piece is that there is a diminishing market for our parents' belongings. Items like maple furniture, and even mahogany, bone china, and leather-bound books, are difficult to get rid of. Younger generations are not as emotionally attached to material possessions as our parents' generation was. They want to minimize their impact on the environment and be free to travel unencumbered or to relocate easily. They are more inclined to buy an inexpensive table from IKEA than to covet a Cushman Colonial.

So one simple step you can take to plan for your future, whether you think you might downsize one day or you just want to spare your children from some of the stressors of becoming a working daughter or son, is to think about what will happen to your stuff. While clearing out a home isn't the most challenging aspect of caregiving, it does take time and sometimes money, and it can also take an emotional toll on both elderly parents and their adult children.

While I could part with the Cushman Colonial furniture, I felt sad and guilty contemplating getting rid of my mother's china tea cups and matching dessert plates. Growing up we used those plates for birthdays, anniversaries, and other celebrations; they had so many memories attached to them. But I finally boxed them up and gave them to the assisted living facility where both of my parents had lived briefly. The staff and residents hold monthly tea parties so I knew the dishes would continue to bring people joy.

Go ahead and ask family and friends if they might want something of yours someday. But let them know that they are under no obligation to store your wedding china for eternity. Give them permission to distribute your belongings to thrift shops, nonprofit organizations, and liquidators if you don't do it on your own. And while you're giving permission for your family to sell the dry sink, give them explicit permission to live their own lives too.

SPARE THE CHILDREN

You can hope that your children, if you have them, will care for you should you need it someday. You can raise them to want to help family but let them know that you want them to live their own lives and that you will appreciate whatever they can do and forgive what they cannot. One working daughter I know has created a mantra, "I won't be stubborn. I will do my best to set myself up for old age. I will be as independent as possible for as long as I can be. I will have a will. I will take medical advice. I will not put my kids through this." Several working daughters have told me they've written letters to their children and plan to deliver them when their children are adults. They don't want their kids to ever feel guilty for prioritizing their lives, their careers, or their families. What a beautiful gesture to share the wisdom of your caregiving experience with your children.

And regardless of whether you have children or not, there are other practical steps you can take now to plan for your future. To begin, think about the same aspects of your life that you have for your parents' lives—health, financial/legal, lifestyle, and end of life—and use the following checklist to get organized.

CHECKLIST FOR AGING

Health

Primary care provider.

If you don't already have a doctor, now is the time to look for one. As you age, you will want to have an established relationship with a primary care physician. Make sure you know what hospital your doctor is affiliated with. If you think you'd prefer to be treated at a different facility, should you need it someday, then consider making a change now.

Checkups and screenings.

Many caregivers let their own health slide while caring for an aging parent. Make a list of the appointments you need to schedule when your caregiving duties let up. When was the last time you had a mammogram? Have you had a colonoscopy? Are you due a visit to the dermatologist or the dentist?

Diet.

If your idea of the four food groups has been sugar, caffeine, carbs, and alcohol, consult a nutritionist or ask your primary care physician for guidance on your diet. It's never too late to make healthy changes.

Exercise.

Get moving! If your only exercise has been running errands, add some more physical activity into your day. Even a few minutes a day adds up. Talk to your doctor about adding strength training to increase muscle and bone strength and yoga or stretching to maintain or improve flexibility. And take heart in the fact that researchers who've studied the caregiver's gain have found many people grow stronger physically as a result of their caregiving responsibilities.

Financial/Legal

Proxies and advanced directives.

Choose your healthcare proxy and fill out your advanced directive. It's never too soon to think about who you trust to make decisions on your behalf should you become unable to. The same goes for completing your own advanced directive. Fill it out before there is a crisis.

Estate planning.

We've talked about how important and helpful it is for your parents to have a will. Well, the same goes for you. If you don't have a will, now is a good time to draft one. If you do have a will, review it. Do you want to change anything?

Retirement funds.

Are you saving enough for retirement? If not, what adjustments do you need to make? Meet with a financial planner if you can afford to. At a minimum, ask to meet with the administrator of your employer's 401K to ensure you are putting away enough money for the future. Many companies offer consultations as part of their benefits program.

Trustees, executors, and powers of attorney.

You've thought about your parents' financial affairs. Now what about your own? Should you appoint a trustee to oversee your assets or a power of attorney? Does it make sense to put your house in a trust? Do you want to purchase long-term care insurance? Is it time to add a relative or a trusted friend to your bank account so that they can help you pay bills should you need the assistance? Just as it's never too late to meet with an eldercare attorney, it's never too early either.

Lifestyle

Housing and location.

When my fifty-five-year-old cousin's children moved out and her husband was nearing retirement, she toured and chose the assisted living facility she plans to move to if and when she can no longer maintain her home. She's so savvy to think ahead. Do you think you will want to maintain a home later in life? Will you want to relocate to be near family or top-ranked hospitals? You don't need to make any decisions before you are ready, but it never hurts to think about your future living arrangements and let family and friends know what you're envisioning.

End of Life

Funeral planning.

Do you have a burial plot? Do you want to be cremated? Can you prepay for your funeral? It's not always the best decision to do so—you may move, or your money might work harder for you in a savings account—but it's helpful to think about your end-of-life plans, including how to pay for them. What kind of service do you think you'll want—a formal remembrance, a religious service, a hootenanny to celebrate your life? Share your vision with family or friends and spare them the guesswork when they are grieving.

LIFE AFTER CAREGIVING

Long-term planning is important to minimize both your own stress as you age and the stress of your family and friends. Shorter-term planning is important too. I know that some days it might feel like you will just be a caregiver until you need a caregiver, but I encourage you to try and embrace other parts of your life even as you're caring for your parents and to plan for your life post-caregiving too. Believe it or not, there *is* more to life than doctor's appointments, errands, and paperwork. And the more proactive you are about embracing the noncaregiving aspects of your life, the more in control you will feel.

I sometimes fantasized about what life with no eldercare obligations would feel like. And it sounded pretty darn great to have a few extra hours every day and to no longer sleep with my cell phone under my pillow in anticipation of a middle of the night emergency. Then I would think about what it would mean if I had no eldercare responsibilities. It would mean I had no parents. And then I would feel sad. And guilty! What kind of a monster wished away their parents? Then I'd feel sad again followed by more uncomfortable guilt. And then I'd just feel defeated, because when you can't even be honest with yourself, how are you supposed to cope?

WE HOLD THESE TWO
TRUTHS TO BE SELF-EVIDENT

However, one of the things I learned from caregiving is that we can hold two truths at the same time. We can look forward to the same thing we are dreading. We can feel both grief when our parent dies and relief that he or she is no longer suffering. I call it grelief. We can eagerly anticipate a time when we won't be hanging out in hospitals, tending to wounds, or managing two households while also feeling sad thinking about when we no longer have our parents with us. And you know what? It's not only normal and healthy to think about a time in the future when you will no longer be a caregiver, it can actually serve as a really powerful planning tool for how you prioritize your life while you are actively caregiving.

Identifying my goals for my life after caregiving helped me create a plan during my time as a caregiver. I knew I wanted, and needed, to be gainfully employed after caregiving, that I wanted my relationships with my husband and children to be intact, and that I wanted to be in good health in order to enjoy my life. Therefore I had to show up at work during my caregiving years, regardless of how tough it got. I had to carve out time for my husband and kids, even when I felt like I had no time or energy. And I couldn't live on Twizzlers, Diet Coke, and Sauvignon Blanc alone; I had to add some vegetables to that diet. And I knew that I wanted to be proud of myself as a daughter when I reflected back on how I had supported my parents, so I let that guide my decisions as their primary support.

When we know what we want, we can take the steps to put it in place. Trying to decide between attending a meeting at work or accompanying a parent to a doctor? When you have a long-term plan, you can run that decision through more than one filter. What's the impact today? What's the longer-term impact?

Here are eight steps to help you plan for life post-caregiving.

Accept where you are.

As we discussed in chapter 1, the first step is always acceptance. Before you can plan for the future, you must accept the present. I hear from working daughters at least once a week that their lives are crumbling as a result of caregiving or that life as they know it is on hold. I get it. I felt the same way as I lost more and more traction and influence at work, argued more frequently with my husband, spent less and less time with my kids, and spent absolutely no time with friends or exercising or eating well. But there is no pause button for life. The reality you awoke to this morning *is* your life. You may not like it. You probably didn't plan it this way. You may never in your wildest dreams have imagined it. But it is your life. You may need to put some things on hold, like a dream vacation you've been saving for or a new job you wanted to apply for, but you cannot put your life on hold. So what? Now what? I'll tell you what: Accept where you are.

Assess your situation.

List the major buckets, or categories, of your life and take an honest assessment of each of them. Some to consider are: health, relationships, career, finances, and personal interests. Your health assessment could look like this: I have always taken good care of myself but lately I've been developing poor habits and letting my doctor's appointments slip. Or I have never prioritized my health and now I'm worried that my bad habits are catching up with me. I'm worried about the effects of caregiving on my physical and mental well-being. Your career assessment might include: I need to become more comfortable using social media tools in order to stay relevant in my job. Or I eventually want to look for a new job but I haven't been networking and maintaining relationships with my contacts.

Set goals.

For each of the categories you identified, think about what you want to have in place, as a baseline, when you are no longer actively caregiving. To continue the examples from earlier, do you need to find a course to learn new skills? You may not be able to commit to a regular class schedule, but you could find an online course and study at your convenience. LinkedIn Learning has thousands of courses in topics like marketing, software development, and accounting. Are you worried you've let your professional network slide? You may not be able to schedule coffee meetings or lunches because you're worried you may need to cancel if you have a caregiving emergency. But you can commit to sending one email a week, or a month, in order to stay connected.

Also think about where you want and need to be financially in the future. If you're not there yet, then what do you need to do now, in three years, in five years, to get there? Where do you want to be career-wise? You may not be able to lean in at work now, but is it wise to lean out? How can you keep one foot in the door so that you can pursue your future goals when the time is right? And note how your career and financial goals are linked. If you are still building your retirement fund, then that may dictate your career plans. If it turns out you cannot afford to downshift at work, then don't. Make the best arrangements you can for your parents' care utilizing paid help if they or you can afford it and social services, siblings, or neighbors if they cannot. Refuse to harbor any guilty feelings about working. Seriously, just reject them if they enter your head. With practice you can learn to let go of guilt. And remember the Working Daughter Bill of Rights: You have the right to earn a living.

Outline the plan.

For each category you have identified, list one to three things you need to do now to make your future goals a reality. You are not allowed to list more than three per category—this is a plan, not a wish list. If your future goal is to find a new job or reenter the workforce if you've taken some time off, then what will you do to ensure that happens? Will you freelance? Work part time? If your goal is to ramp up your career post-caregiving, do you need to have a conversation with your manager? Take a different assignment? If your goal is to maintain or regain your physical health, do you need to schedule workouts or your annual physical? Finally, think about what is feasible to accomplish now during this phase of your life. When you're done, you should have an updated list of your nonnegotiables.

Start where you are.

Don't waste energy thinking about where you were supposed to be at this stage in life or how things were pre-caregiving. Just move forward from here because our lives are what's happening today, not what will happen when caregiving is over. One of the saddest things we can do in life—as a caregiver, or in any situation—is wait until things get better, until someone heals, until work slows down, until we lose weight, or until we find the perfect partner. Our lives are now, not when some future event happens. Living *during* our caregiving experience, instead of holding our breath until it's over, only makes us stronger.

Figure out the shift.

So now that you have a clearer vision for life post-caregiving and how you'll get there, what needs to shift in your life? If your health is a priority, does that mean it is time to stop letting your siblings off the hook so you can take care of you? If maintaining a relationship is a priority, and caregiving is straining that relationship today, then where will you carve out time to invest in people besides the ones you care for? And if work is a priority and you can't afford to lose the job you have, maybe you need to find some help with your caregiving duties so you can focus on your career too. If you run your own company, do you need to find a deputy to keep the business afloat?

A word about recharging your career or reentering the workforce: Two great resources for women reentering work after a break are iRelaunch[2] and ReBootAccel.[3] Both organizations offer conferences to help women hone their skills and develop job search strategies. Both offer one-on-one coaching, and both recognize that it's not just mothers who are on-ramping, it's daughters too.

Think about how you want to feel.

You've identified wants and needs in major categories of your life, now think about your feelings. When you are no longer a caregiver, how will you want to feel? What will you want your caregiving legacy to be? Will you want to know that you made the best choices possible for your family members, and you? Will you want to know that even while you were in the throes of caring for your parent you were still attentive to your children? Will you want to remember that you couldn't be there every minute of every day, maybe because you are a long-distance caregiver or a career-focused caregiver, but when you were there, you were completely present and undistracted? Will you be proud to remember that you set your boundaries? Or that you knew your limitations and therefore asked for help when you needed it so that you didn't get too overwhelmed or frustrated and cranky? As always, there is no right answer. The best answer is the one you come up with when you are honest with yourself. But I will say this: knowing you did your best, whatever your best may be, knowing you were there, whatever there looks like for you, knowing that you operated with integrity, and knowing you were brave and moved through any hesitation, hurt, or fear to be the best caregiver you could in your circumstances is a great way to feel post-caregiving. Plan for it.

Use your future plan as a filter.

Now that you have your plan in place, use it as a filter for making decisions. When you are struggling with prioritizing your own needs with the needs of the person you care for, ask yourself how your decisions will impact you now and in the future. Don't be rigid; a plan after all is only a guide, it's not absolute. But it can be a powerful tool for caring, and living, with intention.

PLANS ARE MEANT TO BE BROKEN

As you make and act on your plans, keep in mind the words of President Dwight Eisenhower: "I have always found that plans are useless, but planning is indispensable." Plans rarely unfold the way we expect them to. Think about it—was caregiving ever in your life plan? The value in developing a plan is in setting the direction for your future. You may not execute the plan perfectly. You may not execute the plan at all because life is full of twists and turns, some positive, some challenging. But in developing a plan, you will get clear about what matters most to you and you will be able to live accordingly, no matter what happens. Without a plan, you may not have that clarity.

Ultimately, planning boils down to articulating your personal value system. Whether you're planning for the long term, establishing goals for the shorter term, or choosing between two competing priorities in real time, it helps to be crystal clear about what you value. And when the time comes, your children and future caregivers will choose their own path in caring, or not, for you. By having thought about your future and shared your vision with the people closest to you, you will give them a tremendous gift. They will understand what matters most to you as they decide what matters most to them. And they then can plan accordingly.

And if you, like many working daughters I know, vow to never put your children through what you've been through as a caregiver, remember this: Yes, eldercare is hard—perhaps one of our most difficult challenges. And yes, it's stressful. Sometimes it's a downright burden. But it is also one of the most rewarding roles we can ever fulfill—to care for someone in his or her most vulnerable moments, to forge a new relationship with our parents different than the child/adult relationship, and to form an emotional connection we didn't know was possible. Why would you shield your family from that?

Chapter Ten

Reflect

"Some things can never be unseen," nurse Jeff said to me.

It was June 2014. Forty hours earlier, I had brought my father to the ER in hopes of having him evaluated because he was forgetful and acting strange. While there he had developed delirium and been given a powerful antipsychotic drug that rendered him incoherent and barely able to walk. Now, as he was awaiting transfer to a hospital closer to where I lived, he was attempting to stand and use the toilet. I could hear the nurse struggling to keep him from falling, so I offered to help.

"Are you sure?" the nurse asked, as he warned me some things could not be erased from my memory.

He was right. Images from my parents' last years flash through my mind from time to time like scenes from a movie. Sometimes the sad memories overwhelm me. I see my father being wheeled out of the hospital that day, so disoriented he didn't even say goodbye to me. I see my mother lying in her hospice bed unable to open her eyes in her final days. I see my daughter hugging her Papa hours before he died. I see me, reflected in the mirror of the bathroom in the United Club at the airport, tears in my eyes, wondering how I was supposed to travel for work when my family needed me at home.

But some of the images I see are happier, or at least bittersweet. I remember eating hamburgers with my father on the patio of his memory care unit. The staff served them "plain, plain, plain," just like he ordered them. I remember having a pizza party with my mother and sisters in the garden of the hospice house, and a "spa day," when I gave my mother a manicure a few weeks before she died. I see me, confident in a board room, winning a new client with a kickass presentation just hours after a frantic visit to the elder law attorney.

And just as some images cannot be unseen, some feelings cannot be unfelt. Grief is a part of my life now, part of my new normal, and I accept it. I accept the fact that I occasionally cry in public, even on the train to New York for business meetings, seated next to a complete stranger talking on his cell phone about "deliverables" and "core competencies."

Songs, scents, television commercials, my kids' accomplishments that I can't share with my parents—all of these can cause my eyes to fill with water quickly and unexpectedly. I tell people to just ignore the tears. "I leak a lot and I'm fine with it," I say. Because I am. Because, although I thought for sure they would at the time, my caregiving experiences didn't break me; they merely changed me. Maybe that butterfly I found in a hospital parking lot at the start of my caregiving crisis was a foreshadowing of my impending metamorphosis.

Back then, I hadn't yet seen the research on the caregiver's gain, the idea that the caregiving experience can provide a number of physiological and psychological benefits (see chapter 1). I hadn't yet interviewed other working daughters whose own experiences supported that research.

Take Simone, a forty-something mother of three, who says of her caregiving experience, "it was the hardest year of my life and about did me in." Simone had to take care of her father who became depressed after her mother was killed in a tragic accident. Simone asked her boss if she could have the flexibility to make her own schedule and then she "worked, parented, and cared practically around the clock." She was exhausted but she believes caregiving made her a better parent and a more effective employee because she became much more deliberate about how she lived her life.

"I no longer live in a world where we say work is work and home is home," she says. "This is a reality—women have young children plus parents, and work. I think it is a good thing for your children to look at you and understand this is a part of life. I don't want them to take away that this is just awful and stressful."

WHAT DOESN'T KILL US
MAKES US STRONGER

The researchers, remember, didn't posit that caregiving isn't stressful; we all know for certain it is. They concluded that caregiving can be both stressful and beneficial to a caregiver and that those two outcomes can be present at the same time. In other words, to cite a popular mantra among family caregivers, what doesn't kill us makes us stronger.

They note that caregiving stress often comes from seeing someone such as your parent suffer, and that will happen whether you care for him or her or not. And they suggest that the antidote to the stress that comes from watching a parent grow old, ill, and eventually die is to take an active role in his or her care.

Stephanie Brown, an assistant professor in internal medicine at the University of Michigan in Ann Arbor, also supports the idea that choosing to care for someone can actually buffer the effects of the stress inherent in caregiving, and she uses basic brain science to prove her theory. In a study published in *Psychological Science*,[1] Brown found that caregivers who spent an average of fourteen or more hours a week caring for someone else lived longer and reduced their risk of dying by about half compared to noncaregivers. Helping others, Brown suggests, can release the hormone oxytocin. Often referred to as the love hormone,[2] oxytocin is controlled by a positive feedback mechanism, so its release causes an action that stimulates more of it.

Brown writes, "Providing help to another person has been hypothesized to promote the physical health of the helper by acting, in part, as a stress buffer. . . . Furthermore, hormones that are causally linked to helping behavior, such as oxytocin, decrease activity of the hypothalamic-pituitary-adrenal (stress) axis and contribute to cellular repair and storage of cell nutrients." Meaning when we assist someone suffering or in need, our brains release a feel-good chemical that reduces future stress.

It's no wonder that, according to a survey by the National Opinion Research Center,[3] 83 percent of the caregivers who responded viewed caregiving as a positive experience. They cite a sense of giving back to someone who has cared for them, the satisfaction of knowing that their loved one is getting excellent care, passing on a tradition of care and modeling caregiving for their children, personal growth, and increased meaning and purpose in one's life as the benefits.

Don't despair if you are currently in the midst of caregiving and you're not seeing or feeling the upside. Many working daughters don't realize the benefits of caregiving while they are busy performing the difficult tasks required of them and trying to balance these added responsibilities with work and possibly marriage and children too. It's when they look back that they see what they have gained from their caregiving experience.

Linda is one such caregiver. Her caregiving experience was incredibly stressful. Two months after she moved away from her family in Minnesota to live in California with her husband, her mother was diagnosed with cancer. Soon Linda was traveling back and forth to Minnesota every six weeks to help, scheduling her trips around her work for a real estate developer in California. And during every trip, her mother would ask her, "Why don't you just stay?"

"I had guilt because I was long distance," she says. "My Dad was always so, so good about making you not feel guilty. 'I want you to have a life of your own,' he'd say. But my mom would say, 'We don't need any [outside] help, the kids can do it.'"

Linda says she tried to help with the emotional part. "I wasn't there to do the hands on that much. But when my father moved into assisted living I talked to him every day. We weren't the type of family that talked every day, but now we were. It started out evening was the best time to call. Then evenings weren't good and I would have to adjust my call time. It was the little things," she says. "All of a sudden you have to adjust your routine. I was so tied to the phone because I wanted to be available." When she was in California, she was on the phone with her family, and when she was in Minnesota, she was on the phone with work.

Sometimes Linda would stay with her parents for two weeks at a time, but the trips got to her. "One [visit home] it was really, really hard and I thought I can't stay one more day. I just needed to go home. I was at my parents' house sleeping on an air mattress and emotionally I just couldn't take it. I incurred the extra cost of changing my flight (even by just one day) but I needed a break. My parents had no idea how I felt. I kept it from them."

After her mother died, Linda's father, who had Parkinson's disease, moved from assisted living to a nursing home. "The worst part," says Linda, "was the distance—hearing in their voice they wanted me there. I got a call about my Dad when I was out of the country. He had fallen and broken a hip."

She got on the next flight and was with her father for five days before he passed. Before he died, her father said to her, "I hope you do something with this gift that you have," noting her skill in caring for her mother and managing the skilled nursing professionals who had cared for him.

"You think about so many things," Linda says, reflecting on the experience. "My father's death left me searching to do more with my life." Shortly after he passed, Linda made a career transition and took a job in administration with a company that provides in-home and respite care to the elderly. "When a former co-worker jokingly suggested that I open a franchise myself, I couldn't get the idea out of my mind," she says. And so she did it.

"If it wasn't for the entire experience I went through with my parents, I wouldn't have the depth of empathy that I have for seniors. I feel like I'm a much better, stronger, more patient, and accepting person," she says. "I've never had anything nearly as emotional as that where I had to call on that strength in my life. I also feel like . . . I love life. Now I feel so much wiser and more accepting. It definitely does feel different."

Linda's experience closely mirrors what the research shows: there is no doubt that stress, exhaustion, and uncertainty come with caregiving. However, while the burden of caring for her parents was significant, the impact on Linda's overall well-being was ultimately positive, even preparing her for a new career. Caregiving can negatively impact your health, your job, and your most important relationships while you are in the thick of it, but that doesn't have to be the end of your caregiving story. It is not the inevitable outcome.

Kelly McGonigal, PhD, a Stanford University health psychologist and author of *The Upside of Stress*, believes that during stressful situations like caregiving, our brains not only produce oxytocin, they also release dopamine, a neurotransmitter that helps us regulate emotional responses and enables us not only to see rewards but to take action to move toward them.

"We are told by the stress reduction industry to soothe ourselves with food, alcohol, binge-watching Netflix, adult coloring books. Some of that's okay, but it's an escape. By turning towards the stress and choosing the activity of caring you can make a connection. And human connection is a mechanism for stress resilience." This may be why some of us choose caregiving in the first place. It may be an instinctual reaction to what we are witnessing.

McGonigal agrees that while caregiving is one of the most common sources of stress, it can also be a great source of resilience. And she says, "Holding these opposites is a skill we need to cultivate. It is possible to feel overwhelmed and empowered at the same time."[4] Two things can be true at once.

So how do we cultivate that skill? How can we realize the caregiver's gain, not only post caregiving, but while we are still providing care? We can start by reflecting on our caregiving situation as we are experiencing it, and of course after too.

The Journal of Humanistic Psychology defines reflection as the process of "examining and exploring an issue of concern, triggered by an experience, which creates and clarifies meaning in terms of self, and which results in a changed conceptual perspective."[5] Reflection during caregiving can help us identify and make sense of the myriad emotions we are experiencing. By reflecting we discover that caregiving ultimately doesn't break us down, it builds us up. Our careers aren't ruined, they're at an inflection point—as was the case with Linda. Aging, illness, and death can reveal wisdom, beauty, and peace.

THE STORIES WE TELL

Storytelling is a powerful tool for self-reflection. Each of us creates a narrative about our own lives, whether we are aware of it or not. And these stories we tell ourselves matter. They influence how we perceive ourselves and the world, and they can have a substantial impact on our psychological and physical health.[6] Be conscious of the story you are writing. Own it. It will help you understand not just where you've been, but where you want to go from there. As the writer Nora Ephron said in her commencement address to Wellesley College, "Above all, be the heroine of your life, not the victim."[7]

FOUR STEPS TO CREATING AND REFLECTING ON YOUR CAREGIVING STORY

Do you know your story? Find a quiet place and reflect on the following questions honestly and with no judgment. Your answers will help reveal the story you are telling. If you don't like it, write a new chapter!

Setting

What is your caregiving story? Describe your experience. When did it start? What happened? How did it end or what is the present-day situation?

Character

What is your role in the story? What do you do? What do you choose not to do? Who else is involved? How do you interact with them? What are you good at? With what do you struggle?

Plot

What is challenging about the situation? What is good? What skills did you use? What new skills have you developed? Have you formed any new relationships? Have you ended any relationships? What parts of the story do you want to forget? What parts of the story would you want to relive?

Resolution

Based on what you've seen, what you've done, and what you now know, what do you want to continue doing in your life? What do you want to stop doing? What do you want to start doing? And finally, what actions do you have to take in support of your next chapter?

THE POWER OF STORIES

Abby, the woman who brought her mother to live with her from out of state, crafted a positive and powerful caregiving story, and as a result she was able to see the upside to almost every situation she faced.

An event manager, she had to make some changes at work to accommodate her new caregiving role when her mother came to stay. "Luckily, I have one of those jobs and workplaces—I have all kinds of flexible options. If I work Saturdays or Sundays, it's an unwritten policy, but I can take comp time. And because most of the events are at night, my office hours don't have to be the same as everyone else's."

When she noticed some inequities in how management supported working parents versus how they supported working daughters and sons, she worked to effect positive change. "I have brought some things to [management's] attention that wasn't on their radar or a concern for them. There are a lot of people with kids and always the attitude has been if the kid is sick and you've got to go to the doctor, everyone is cool with that. If you have a spouse, you can work nights with no issue. But I have to pay to work after 9." Abby hired home health aides to stay with her mother when she was at work. Her managers hadn't realized that until Abby pointed it out. "If an aide cancels, I'm stuck."

And when Abby reflected on her experiences and what she had learned as a caregiver, she decided she wanted to help other working daughters. She now runs a consulting business on the side and offers educational sessions and private consultations to help other caregivers create care plans and find qualified aides to assist their parents.

And to support all that she does, Abby prioritizes self-care. "I have realized that I have to fight for me as hard as I fight for other people. I have to cook healthy for Mommy and for me. I know I won't be a caregiver forever. That's why I work out."

Like Abby, Chryssa also cared for her mother. She was the daughter who took her mother to adorn family graves with flowers. But unlike Abby, Chryssa was not taking care of herself. The story she was telling herself was that she was not doing enough.

"My doctor started saying, 'You are stressing yourself out. I am more worried about your health than your mother's—and she has dementia. My kids were saying, 'Mom we're going to be going to your funeral if you stress yourself out.'"

But Chryssa's mother and even a close girlfriend tried to make her feel guilty about putting her mother in assisted living. "My mother was taking on the role of the parent who says, 'If you loved me . . .' For a while there I didn't want to answer the phone. Some of it was my mother just wanting attention. It becomes a psychological game."

Chryssa decided in order to protect her own health she would no longer allow her mother to make her feel guilty. "She was still okay. She was still functioning. So I decided to protect myself from guilt. Now when my mother says, 'If you loved me . . .' I tell her, 'If I didn't love you I wouldn't be here at all." Chryssa changed her story and in the new version she says, "I am doing all that I am able to physically, mentally, and financially."

"There's no law that says you need to give up your life," she says. "In fact, if you want to honor someone's end of life, live the one you have." I couldn't agree more.

MY NEXT CHAPTER

After my father died in July 2017, I felt this sense of freedom I hadn't experienced in years. It felt strange to have time for myself, but I got used to it just like I got used to not worrying if my phone was fully charged at night, used to not waking up and immediately thinking about how I could fit a visit with my father into my schedule, used to not pretending to be in my home office when I was actually in a doctor's office, a memory care unit, or pulled over on the side of the road working.

I think my boss thought I would throw myself back into my work, show a renewed commitment and energy—and I had always thought I would too. But I didn't. I avoided work travel when I could and I only did what was required of me. I wasn't interested in working long hours and weekends or missing a night at home with my husband and kids. I had already missed too many.

Meanwhile the business was facing some challenges—a shifting marketplace and more competition. My peers on the management team were talking about "doing whatever it takes" and "giving 110 percent" to win new business and get us through the tough times. But I wasn't willing to do more than I was already—working about forty-five hours per week. For three years I had done whatever it took just to show up to work while dealing with the challenges my family faced. And while my company had provided me the flexibility I needed, I was feeling the effects of the flexibility stigma. I still had a "seat at the table" on the management team, but I could tell my opinion didn't carry the same weight and influence it once had. And one day, when a coworker told me she didn't feel she could count on me and cited an example of a deadline I had missed when my mother was on hospice—years earlier— I knew I might never shake my reputation as the one whose family life is always impacting her work.

I was feeling burned out. I had fought with everything in me to free my father from a psych ward and place him in a good nursing home. I had stood witness as my mother made peace with her life choices. I had comforted my children as they said goodbye to their grandparents. I had held the hand of people I loved as they transitioned from life to death. Those things were what mattered, not landing another account.

I wanted to use my skills to do more work that mattered, so I applied and was accepted into two different programs for entrepreneurs. I didn't know exactly what I would do next, just that I wanted to build something meaningful that would support other working daughters as they were balancing elder-care, career, and life. And I continued to work at the "day job" because I had to pay the bills.

Then in February 2018, my company cut my hours as part of a staff reduction. I was disappointed but not surprised. Choice. Consequence. A week later, my fifty-one-year-old husband was diagnosed with pancreatic cancer and suddenly I was a caregiver once more.

While caring for a spouse is different than caring for a parent, many things were the same. I had to accept that this was our life now. I had to prioritize—quit the entrepreneurial program, focus on my husband, care for, protect, and love my kids, and drive them all over town. Teenagers! I had to prepare for the worst while still focusing on what was good in my life. And once again, I had to figure out how to keep my job at a time when I was busy, tired, distracted, and, quite frankly, terrified because I needed a paycheck and health insurance now more than ever.

A few months after the diagnosis, my husband was handling his chemo-therapy treatments well and life felt manageable, at least for the time being. At work, we were winning business and the firm was growing again. My boss scheduled a call to talk about my job.

"I'm not sure you're really happy in your current role," she said. "If you were to describe your dream job, what would it be?"

"Really?" I wanted to say. "I am fifty-one, my husband is sick, and I have two kids to put through college. I don't give a rat's ass if I run the company or sweep the floors. I just want to feel secure and valued."

Of course I didn't say that. I made up some bullshit answer because I felt desperate. But in thinking about that question and reflecting on how I responded to it, I discovered my next chapter and I changed my story. I was no longer going to tell myself the story of the woman whose career took a hit as a result of her caregiving. I was going to tell a story about a woman who adds value—value to her employer, value to her family, and value to other working daughters.

I may not have the same enthusiasm for my marketing job as I once did, but I take pride in doing quality work that adds value to the firm. I don't know what my next career move will be, but I do know it will involve making sure the world values the work of caring. And I have no idea what the future holds for my family, but I know that where I add the most value is at home, caring for them. And that realization is my caregiver's gain.

Notes

INTRODUCTION

1. National Alliance for Caregiving and AARP, "Caregiving in the U.S.," June 2015, https://www.aarp.org/content/dam/aarp/ppi/2015/caregiving-in-the-united-states-2015-report-revised.pdf.

2. Caregiving.org, "The Metlife Juggling Act Study: Balancing Caregiving with Work and the Costs Involved," MetLife Mature Market Institute, National Alliance for Caregiving, and the National Center on Women and Aging, November 1999, http://www.caregiving.org/data/jugglingstudy.pdf.

1. ACCEPT

1. "Baby Boomers Retire," Pew Research, December 29, 2010, http://www.pewresearch.org/fact-tank/2010/12/29/baby-boomers-retire/.

2. "FastStats," National Center for Health Statistics, Centers for Disease Control and Prevention, accessed October 30, 2018, https://www.cdc.gov/nchs/fastats/life-expectancy.htm.

3. Jennifer M. Ortman, Victoria A. Velkoff, and Howard Hogan, "An Aging Nation: The Older Population in the United States," United States Census Bureau, May 2014, https://www.census.gov/prod/2014pubs/p25-1140.pdf.

4. Donald Redfoot, Lynn Feinberg, and Ari Houser, "The Aging of the Baby Boom and the Growing Care Gap: A Look at Future Declines in the Availability of Family Caregivers," AARP Public Policy Institute, https://www.aarp.org/content/dam/aarp/research/public_policy_institute/ltc/2013/baby-boom-and-the-growing-care-gap-insight-AARP-ppi-ltc.pdf.

5. Beth Baker, "Improving Paid Caregivers' Work Lives," *Next Avenue*, April 15, 2015, https://www.nextavenue.org/improving-paid-caregivers-work-lives/.

6. "Basic Statistics About Home Care," The National Association for Home Care and Hospice, 2010, http://www.nahc.org/assets/1/7/10hc_stats.pdf.

7. Juliette Cubanski and Tricia Neuman, "10 Essential Facts About Medicare's Financial Outlook," Henry J. Kaiser Family Foundation, February 2, 2017, https://www.kff.org/medicare/issue-brief/10-essential-facts-about-medicares-financial-outlook/.

8. Redfoot, Feinberg, and Houser, "The Aging of the Baby Boom and the Growing Care Gap."

9. National Alliance for Caregiving and AARP, "Caregiving in the U.S.," June 2015, https://www.aarp.org/content/dam/aarp/ppi/2015/caregiving-in-the-united-states-2015-report-revised.pdf.

10. Lynn Feinberg, Susan C. Reinhard, Ari Houser, and Rita Choula, "Valuing the Invaluable: 2011 Update The Growing Contributions and Costs of Family Caregiving," AARP Public Policy Institute, https://assets.aarp.org/rgcenter/ppi/ltc/i51-caregiving.pdf.

11. Christina Ianzito, "The Hidden Male Caregiver," AARP, accessed October 30, 2018, https://www.aarp.org/caregiving/life-balance/info-2017/hidden-male-caregiver.html.

12. "Caregiving in the U.S."

13. "Caregivers of Older Adults: A Focused Look at Those Caring for Someone Age 50+," AARP, June 2015, https://www.aarp.org/content/dam/aarp/ppi/2015/caregivers-of-older-adults-focused-look.pdf.

14. "2018 Alzheimer's Disease Fact and Figures," Alzheimer's Association, https://www.alz.org/media/HomeOffice/Facts%20and%20Figures/facts-and-figures.pdf.

15. "Caregiving in the U.S."

16. "Work and Eldercare," Family Caregiver Alliance, accessed October 30, 2018, https://www.caregiver.org/work-and-eldercare.

17. "Caregiving in the U.S."

18. "Caregiving in the U.S."

19. "Caregiving in the U.S."

20. Lynn Feinberg and Rita Choula, "Understanding the Impact of Work and Family Caregiving," AARP Public Policy Institute, accessed October 30, 2018, https://www.aarp.org/content/dam/aarp/research/public_policy_institute/ltc/2012/understanding-impact-family-caregiving-work-AARP-ppi-ltc.pdf.

21. "Pay Equity and Discrimination," The Institute for Women's Policy, Research, accessed October 30, 2018, https://iwpr.org/issue/employment-education-economic-change/pay-equity-discrimination/.

22. "Life Expectancy at Birth and at Age 65," Centers for Disease Control and Protections, accessed October 31, 2018, https://www.cdc.gov/nchs/data/hus/2017/006.pdf.

23. Charlotte Alter, "11 Surprising Facts About Women and Poverty From the Shriver Report," *Time*, January 13, 2014, http://time.com/2026/11-surprising-facts-about-women-and-poverty-from-the-shriver-report/.

24. Ira Rosofsky, PhD, "Caregiver Stress: Would You Like Some Angst with That Sandwich Generation?" *Psychology Today*, April 12, 2009, https://www.psychologytoday.com/us/blog/adventures-in-old-age/200904/caregiver-stress-would-you-some-angst-sandwich-generation.

25. "Caregiving in the U.S."

26. Betty J. Kramer, PhD, "Gain in the Caregiving Experience: Where Are We? What Next?" *The Gerontologist* 37 (1997): 218–32.

27. Paula Span, "Caregiving's Hidden Benefits," *New York Times*, October 12, 2011, https://newoldage.blogs.nytimes.com/2011/10/12/caregivings-hidden-benefits/?mtrref=www.google.com.

28. David L. Roth, PhD, Lisa Fredman, PhD, and William E. Haley, "Informal Caregiving and Its Impact on Health: A Reappraisal from Population-Based Studies," *The Gerontologist* 55, no. 2 (April 1, 2015): 309–19, https://doi.org/10.1093/geront/gnu177.

3. PRIORITIZE

1. Caring.com, "80% of Caregivers Report Strain on Their Marriages," February 5, 2009, https://www.caring.com/about/news-room/press-release-caregiver-marital-stress.

2. National Alliance for Caregiving and AARP, "Caregiving in the U.S.," June 2015, https://www.aarp.org/content/dam/aarp/ppi/2015/caregiving-in-the-united-states-2015-report-revised.pdf.

3. Centers for Disease Control and Prevention, "QuickStats: Percentage of Adults Who Often Felt Very Tired or Exhausted in the Past 3 Months,* by Sex and Age Group—National Health Interview Survey, United States, 2010–2011," April 12, 2013, https://www.cdc.gov/mmwr/preview/mmwrhtml/mm6214a5.htm.

4. U.S. Bureau of Labor Statistics, "American Time Use Survey," last modified December 20, 2016, https://www.bls.gov/tus/charts/household.htm.

5. "American Time Use Survey."

6. U.S. Bureau of Labor Statistics, "Volunteering in the United States, 2015," February 25, 2016, https://www.bls.gov/news.release/volun.nr0.htm.

7. "American Time Use Survey."

8. Katie Johnston, "Nearly 1 in 4 US Workers Go Without Paid Time Off," *Boston Globe*, August 14, 2014, https://www.bostonglobe.com/business/2014/08/13/one-few-countries-that-doesn-mandate-paid-vacation-time/eqodEqumohPyca5kt6hrZO/story.html.

4. FLEX

1. Meghan Casserly, "Forbes Woman and TheBump.Com 'Parenthood and Economy 2012' Survey Results," *Forbes*, September 12, 2012, https://www.forbes.com/sites/meghancasserly/2012/09/12/forbeswoman-and-thebump-com-parenthood-and-economy-2012-survey-results/#313ed5c83212.

2. Mitra Toossi and Teresa L. Morisi, "Women in the Workforce Before, During, and After the Great Recession," U.S. Bureau of Labor Statistics, July 2017, https://www.bls.gov/spotlight/2017/women-in-the-workforce-before-during-and-after-the-great-recession/pdf/women-in-the-workforce-before-during-and-after-the-great-recession.pdf.

3. Alex Mahadevan, "Women Are Leaving the Workforce at a Staggering Rate," *AOL*, August 23, 2017, https://www.aol.com/article/finance/2017/08/23/women-are-leaving-the-workforce-at-a-staggering-rate-heres-why/23159057/.

4. U.S. Bureau of Labor Statistics, "93 Percent of Managers and 46 Percent of Service Workers Had Paid Sick Leave Benefits in March 2017," *TED: The Economics Daily*, August 2, 2017, https://www.bls.gov/opub/ted/2017/93-percent-of-managers-and-46-percent-of-service-workers-had-paid-sick-leave-benefits-in-march-2017.htm.

5. Emma Plumb, "Take 5: Stanford Economist Nicholas Bloom on the Business Case for Telecommuting," 1 Million for Work Flexibility, accessed October 30, 2018, https://www.workflexibility.org/take-five-stanford-economist-nicholas-bloom-business-case-telecommuting.

6. Vodafone, "Vodafone Global Survey Reveals Rapid Adoption of Flexible Working," February 8, 2016, https://www.vodafone.com/content/index/media/vodafone-group-releases/2016/flexible-working-survey.html#.

7. M. Pitts-Catsouphes, C. Matz-Costa, and E. Besen, "Age and Generations. Understanding Experiences in the Workplace," Research Highlight 6, The Sloan Center on Aging and Work, Boston College, March 2009, https://www.bc.edu/content/dam/files/research_sites/agingandwork/pdf/publications/RH06_Age_Generations.pdf.

8. Tara Siegel Bernard, "The Unspoken Stigma of Workplace Flexibility," *New York Times*, June 4, 2013, https://www.nytimes.com/2013/06/15/your-money/the-unspoken-stigma-of-workplace-flexibility.html.

9. Deloitte, "Deloitte Announces 16 Weeks of Fully Paid Family Leave Time for Caregiving," September 8, 2016, https://www2.deloitte.com/us/en/pages/about-deloitte/articles/press-releases/deloitte-announces-sixteen-weeks-of-fully-paid-family-leave-time-for-caregiving.html.

10. Walmart, "Working at Walmart. Opportunities and Benefits," accessed October 30, 2018, https://corporate.walmart.com/our-story/working-at-walmart.

11. Transamerica Center for Retirement Studies, "Striking Similarities and Disconcerting Disconnects: Employers, Workers and Retirement Security 18th Annual Transamerica Retire-

ment Survey," August 2018, https://www.transamericacenter.org/docs/default-source/retirement-survey-of-employers/tcrs2018_sr_employer-retirement-research.pdf.

12. Emmie Martin, "Here's How Much Money American Women Earn at Every Age," *CNBC*, September 12, 2017, https://www.cnbc.com/2017/09/12/heres-how-much-money-american-women-earn-at-every-age.html.

13. Teresa Ghilarducci, "Why Women Over 50 Can't Find Jobs," *PBS*, January 14, 2016, https://www.pbs.org/newshour/economy/women-over-50-face-cant-find-jobs.

14. Brenda Flinn, "Millennials: The Emerging Generation of Family Caregivers," *AARP*, May 22, 2018, https://www.aarp.org/ppi/info-2018/millennial-family-caregiving.html.

15. Federal Reserve Bank of St. Louis, "Long-Term Unemployment Affected Older Women Most Following Recession," November 17, 2015, https://www.stlouisfed.org/on-the-economy/2015/november/older-women-recession-long-term-unemployment.

16. JoAnn Jenkins, "Caregiving Costly to Family Caregivers," *AARP*, https://www.aarp.org/caregiving/financial-legal/info-2017/family-caregiving-costly-jj.html.

17. Kara Baskin, "Female Executives Discuss How Motherhood Has Helped Them on the Job," *Boston Globe*, October 4, 2017, https://www.bostonglobe.com/magazine/2017/10/24/female-executives-discuss-how-motherhood-has-helped-them-job/EkT2i2aAVZaSpC1PqjZmyI/story.html.

18. MetLife, "U.S. Business Loses from $17.1 Billion to $33.6 Billion Per Year in Productivity for Caregivers Who Take Time from Their Work Responsibilities; Online Calculator Available for Employers to Determine Costs," July 11, 2006, https://www.businesswire.com/news/home/20060711005250/en/U.S.-Business-Loses-17.1-Billion-33.6-Billion.

19. AfterEllen.com, The Linster, "Variations on Your Theme (Song)," July 14, 2008, https://www.afterellen.com/general-news/34691-variations-on-your-theme-song#3tdBe0lgoPhjRrD-Z.99.

5. CHOOSE

1. The White House, "Presidential Proclamation—National Family Caregivers Month, 2016," October 31, 2016, https://obamawhitehouse.archives.gov/the-press-office/2016/10/31/presidential-proclamation-national-family-caregivers-month-2016.

2. Robin Seaton Jefferson, "New Survey Finds Adult Children Want Their Parents to Age at Home," *Forbes*, August 20, 2017, https://www.forbes.com/sites/robinseatonjefferson/2017/04/30/new-survey-finds-adult-children-want-their-parents-to-age-at-home/#15c72bffb44b.

3. Centers for Disease Control and Prevention, National Center for Injury Prevention and Control, Web-Based Injury Statistics Query and Reporting System (WISQARS) [online], accessed August 5, 2016, https://www.cdc.gov/injury/wisqars/.

6. MANAGE

1. Shelley Raffin Bouchal, RN, PhD, Lillian Rallison, RN, PhD, Nancy J. Moules, RN, PhD, and Shane Sinclair, PhD, "Holding On and Letting Go: Families' Experiences of Anticipatory Mourning in Terminal Cancer," University of Calgary, March 10, 2015, https://doi.org/10.1177/0030222815574700.

2. U.S. Department of Veteran Affairs, "Veterans," accessed October 30, 2018, https://www.benefits.va.gov/persona/veteran-elderly.asp.

3. PwC, "Formal Cost of Long-Term Care Services: How Can Society Meet a Growing Need?" accessed October 30, 2018, https://www.pwc.com/us/en/industries/insurance/library/long-term-care-services.html.

4. Peter Dizikes, "3 Questions: Joseph Coughlin on Innovation for an Aging Population," *MIT News*, November 8, 2017, http://news.mit.edu/2017/3-questions-joseph-coughlin-innovation-aging-population-1108.

5. Mark Busch, "How to Preplan Your Funeral," *Busch*, March 26, 2016, https://www.buschcares.com/blog/how-to-preplan-your-funeral.

6. Lawrence R. Samuel, PhD, "Americans in General Are Uncomfortable Thinking About Death," *Psychology Today*, June 23, 2015.

7. DISRUPT

1. Clayton M. Christensen, Michael E. Raynor, and Rory McDonald, "What Is Disruptive Innovation?" *Harvard Business Review*, December 2015, https://hbr.org/2015/12/what-is-disruptive-innovation.

2. AARP, "New State Law to Help Family Caregivers," *AARP*, accessed October 30, 2018, https://www.aarp.org/politics-society/advocacy/caregiving-advocacy/info-2014/aarp-creates-model-state-bill.html.

3. Jonathan Woetzel, Anu Madgavkar, Kweilin Ellingrud, Eric Labaye, Sandrine Devillard, Eric Kutcher, James Manyika, Richard Dobbs, and Mekala Krishnan, "How Advancing Women's Equality Can Add $12 Trillion to Global Growth," McKinsey Global Report, September 2015, https://www.mckinsey.com/featured-insights/employment-and-growth/how-advancing-womens-equality-can-add-12-trillion-to-global-growth.

4. Howard Gleckman, "A New Snapshot of America's 44 Million Family Caregivers: Who They Are and What They Do," *Forbes*, June 4, 2015, https://www.forbes.com/sites/howardgleckman/2015/06/04/a-new-snapshot-of-americas-44-million-family-caregivers-who-they-are-and-what-they-do/#4907e3bf3ab2.

5. L. M. Rossen, M. J. K. Osterman, B. E. Hamilton, and J. A. Martin, "Quarterly Provisional Estimates for Selected Birth Indicators, 2016–Quarter 1, 2018," National Center for Health Statistics, National Vital Statistics System, Vital Statistics Rapid Release Program, 2018, https://www.cdc.gov/nchs/nvss/vsrr/natality-dashboard.htm.

6. Heidi Hartmann, PhD, Jeff Hayes, PhD, Rebecca Huber, Kelly Rolfes-Haase, and Jooyeoun Suh, PhD, "The Shifting Supply and Demand of Care Work: The Growing Role of People of Color and Immigrants," Institute for Women's Policy Research, June 27, 2018.

7. U.S. Department of Labor Wage and Hour Division, "Fact Sheet #25: Home Health Care and the Companionship Services Exemption Under the Fair Labor Standards Act (FLSA)," September 2013, https://www.dol.gov/whd/regs/compliance/whdfs25.pdf.

8. RENEW

1. Sinead Brady, "Self-Care Can Make You More Successful at Work," *Image*, January 23, 2018, https://www.image.ie/business/self-care-can-make-successful-work.

2. Audra Lorde, *A Burst of Light and Other Essays* (Ithaca, NY: Firebrand Books, 1988).

3. "Fifteen Benefits of Drinking Water," *Medical News Today*, July 16, 2018, https://www.medicalnewstoday.com/articles/290814.php.

4. "Dietary Reference Intakes: Water, Potassium, Sodium, Chloride, and Sulfate," The National Academies of Sciences, Engineering, Medicine, February 11, 2014, http://www.nationalacademies.org/hmd/Reports/2004/Dietary-Reference-Intakes-Water-Potassium-Sodium-Chloride-and-Sulfate.aspx.

5. C. Thøgersen-Ntoumani, E. A. Loughren, F. E. Kinnafick, I. M. Taylor, J. L. Duda, and K. R. Fox, "Changes in Work Affect in Response to Lunchtime Walking in Previously Physically Inactive Employees: A Randomized Trial," *Scandinavian Journal of Medicine and Science in Sports*, December 2015, https://www.ncbi.nlm.nih.gov/pubmed/25559067.

6. "Cold Weather Fitness Guide," American Heart Association, accessed October 30, 2018, https://www.heart.org/idc/groups/heart-public/@wcm/@fc/documents/downloadable/ucm_457235.pdf.

7. Mayo Clinic, "Exercise and Stress: Get Moving to Manage Stress," accessed October 30, 2018, https://www.mayoclinic.org/healthy-lifestyle/stress-management/in-depth/exercise-and-stress/art-20044469.

8. "Take A Nap! Change Your Life," Sara Mednick, accessed October 30, 2018, https://www.saramednick.com.

9. Girija Kaimal, Kendra Ray, and Juan Muniz, "Reduction of Cortisol Levels and Participants' Responses Following Art Making," May 23, 2016, https://www.tandfonline.com/doi/full/10.1080/07421656.2016.1166832.

10. "It's Official—Spending Time Outside Is Good for You," University of East Anglia, June 7, 2018, https://www.uea.ac.uk/about/-/it-s-official-spending-time-outside-is-good-for-you.

11. Bridget Murray, "Writing to Heal," *American Psychological Association* 33, no. 6 (June 2002), https://www.apa.org/monitor/jun02/writing.aspx.

12. Michael J. Breus, PhD, "Yoga Can Help with Insomnia," *Psychology Today*, October 4, 2012, https://www.psychologytoday.com/us/blog/sleep-newzzz/201210/yoga-can-help-insomnia.

13. Kimberly Sena Moore, PhD, "Why Listening to Music Makes Us Feel Good," *Psychology Today*, January 20, 2011, https://www.psychologytoday.com/us/blog/your-musical-self/201101/why-listening-music-makes-us-feel-good.

14. Mayo Clinic, "Massage Therapy," August 10, 2017, https://www.mayoclinic.org/tests-procedures/massage-therapy/about/pac-20384595.

15. R. J. Davidson, J. Kabat-Zinn, J. Schumacher, M. Rosenkranz, D. Muller, S. F. Santorelli, F. Urbanowski, A. Harrington, K. Bonus, and J. F. Sheridan, "Alterations in Brain and Immune Function Produced by Mindfulness Meditation," *Psychosomatic Medicine*, 2003, https://www.ncbi.nlm.nih.gov/pubmed/12883106.

16. Mayo Clinic, "Support Groups: Make Connections, Get Help," June 26, 2018, https://www.mayoclinic.org/healthy-lifestyle/stress-management/in-depth/support-groups/art-20044-655.

17. Robert Emmons, "Why Gratitude Is Good," *Greater Good Magazine*, Greater Good Science Center at UC Berkeley, November 16, 2010, https://greatergood.berkeley.edu/article/item/why_gratitude_is_good.

18. Danny Lewis, "Feeling Down? Scientists Say Cooking and Baking Could Help You Feel Better," *Smithsonian Magazine*, November 29, 2016, https://www.smithsonianmag.com/smart-news/feeling-down-scientists-say-cooking-and-baking-may-help-you-feel-better-18096-1223/#JyQLW7SzTJ7Oku25.99.

19. Kim Fredericks, "Here's What You Need to Know About the Health Benefits of Chocolate," *Reader's Digest*, accessed October 30, 2018, https://www.rd.com/health/wellness/health-benefits-of-chocolate/.

20. Agnes E. Van Den Berg and Mariëtte H. G. Custers, "Gardening Promotes Neuroendocrine and Affective Restoration from Stress," *Journal of Health Psychology*, June 3, 2010, http://journals.sagepub.com/doi/10.1177/1359105310365577.

21. Holly B. Shakya and Nicholas A. Christakis, "A New, More Rigorous Study Confirms: The More You Use Facebook, the Worse You Feel," *Harvard Business Review*, April 10, 2017, https://hbr.org/2017/04/a-new-more-rigorous-study-confirms-the-more-you-use-facebook-the-worse-you-feel.

22. Stacy Horn, "Singing Changes Your Brain: Group Singing Has Been Scientifically Proven to Lower Stress, Relieve Anxiety, and Elevate Endorphins," *Time*, August 16, 2013, http://ideas.time.com/2013/08/16/singing-changes-your-brain/.

23. M. Stromback, M. Wiklund, E. S. Renberg, and E. B. Malmgren-Olsson, "Complex Symptomatology among Young Women Who Present with Stress-Related Problems," *Scandinavian Journal of Caring Sciences* 29, no. 2 (2015): 234–47, https://www.ncbi.nlm.nih.gov/pubmed/24953100.

24. American Dental Association, "Federal Government, ADA Emphasize Importance of Flossing and Interdental Cleaners," August 4, 2016, https://www.ada.org/en/press-room/news-releases/2016-archive/august/statement-from-the-american-dental-association-about-inter-dental-cleaners.

9. PLAN

1. Richard Eisenberg, "Sorry, Nobody Wants Your Parents' Stuff," *Next Avenue*, February 9, 2017, www.nextavenue.org.
2. iRelaunch, https://www.irelaunch.com.
3. ReBootAccel, https://rebootaccel.com.

10. REFLECT

1. Stephanie L. Brown, Dylan M. Smith, Richard Schulz, Mohammed U. Kabeto, Peter A. Ubel, Michael Poulin, Jaehee Yi, Catherine Kim, and Kenneth M. Langa, "Caregiving Behavior Is Associated with Decreased Mortality Risk," *Psychological Science*, April 20, 2009, https://www.ncbi.nlm.nih.gov/pmc/articles/PMC2865652/.
2. Markus MacGill, "What Is the Link between Love and Oxytocin?" *Medical News Today*, September 4, 2017, https://www.medicalnewstoday.com/articles/275795.php.
3. American Psychological Association, "Positive Aspects of Caregiving," May 2014, https://www.apa.org/pi/about/publications/caregivers/faq/positive-aspects.aspx.
4. Interview with author, March 21, 2016.
5. Evelyn M. Boyd and Ann W. Fales, "Reflective Learning Key to Learning from Experience," *Journal of Humanistic Psychology*, April 1, 1983, https://doi.org/10.1177/0022167883232011.
6. Sherry Hamby, PhD, "Resilience and . . . 4 Benefits to Sharing Your Story," *Psychology Today*, September 3, 2013, https://www.psychologytoday.com/us/blog/the-web-violence/201309/resilience-and-4-benefits-sharing-your-story.
7. Nora Ephron, "'62 Addressed the Graduates in 1996," Wellesley College Commencement Archives, https://www.wellesley.edu/events/commencement/archives/1996commencement.

Bibliography

INTRODUCTION

Caregiving.org. "The Metlife Juggling Act Study: Balancing Caregiving with Work and the Costs Involved." MetLife Mature Market Institute, National Alliance for Caregiving, and the National Center on Women and Aging, November 1999. http://www.caregiving.org/data/jugglingstudy.pdf.

Frost, Robert. *North of Boston*. New York: Henry Holt, 1915; Bartleby.com, 1999. www.bartleby.com/118/.

National Alliance for Caregiving and AARP. "Caregiving in the U.S." June 2015. https://www.aarp.org/content/dam/aarp/ppi/2015/caregiving-in-the-united-states-2015-report-revised.pdf.

CHAPTER 1

"2018 Alzheimer's Disease Fact and Figures." Alzheimer's Association. https://www.alz.org/media/HomeOffice/Facts%20and%20Figures/facts-and-figures.pdf.

Alter, Charlotte. "11 Surprising Facts About Women and Poverty From the Shriver Report." *Time*, January 13, 2014. http://time.com/2026/11-surprising-facts-about-women-and-poverty-from-the-shriver-report/.

"Baby Boomers Retire." Pew Research, December 29, 2010. http://www.pewresearch.org/fact-tank/2010/12/29/baby-boomers-retire/.

Baker, Beth. "Improving Paid Caregivers' Work Lives." *Next Avenue*, April 15, 2015. https://www.nextavenue.org/improving-paid-caregivers-work-lives/.

"Basic Statistics About Home Care." The National Association for Home Care and Hospice, 2010. http://www.nahc.org/assets/1/7/10hc_stats.pdf.

"Caregivers of Older Adults: A Focused Look at Those Caring for Someone Age 50+." AARP, June 2015. https://www.aarp.org/content/dam/aarp/ppi/2015/caregivers-of-older-adults-focused-look.pdf.

Cubanski, Juliette, and Tricia Neuman. "10 Essential Facts About Medicare's Financial Outlook." Henry J. Kaiser Family Foundation, February 2, 2017. https://www.kff.org/medicare/issue-brief/10-essential-facts-about-medicares-financial-outlook/.

"FastStats." National Center for Health Statistics, Centers for Disease Control and Prevention. Accessed October 30, 2018. https://www.cdc.gov/nchs/fastats/life-expectancy.htm.

Feinberg, Lynn, and Rita Choula. "Understanding the Impact of Work and Family Caregiving." AARP Public Policy Institute. Accessed October 30, 2018. https://www.aarp.org/content/dam/aarp/research/public_policy_institute/ltc/2012/understanding-impact-family-caregiving-work-AARP-ppi-ltc.pdf.

Feinberg, Lynn, Susan C. Reinhard, Ari Houser, and Rita Choula. "Valuing the Invaluable: 2011 Update The Growing Contributions and Costs of Family Caregiving." AARP Public Policy Institute. https://assets.aarp.org/rgcenter/ppi/ltc/i51-caregiving.pdf.

Ianzito, Christina. "The Hidden Male Caregiver." AARP. Accessed October 30, 2018. https://www.aarp.org/caregiving/life-balance/info-2017/hidden-male-caregiver.html.

Kramer, Betty J., PhD. "Gain in the Caregiving Experience: Where Are We? What Next?" *The Gerontologist* 37 (1997): 218–32.

"Life Expectancy at Birth and at Age 65." Centers for Disease Control and Protections. Accessed October 31, 2018. https://www.cdc.gov/nchs/data/hus/2017/006.pdf.

National Alliance for Caregiving and AARP. "Caregiving in the U.S." June 2015. https://www.aarp.org/content/dam/aarp/ppi/2015/caregiving-in-the-united-states-2015-report-revised.pdf.

Ortman, Jennifer M., Victoria A. Velkoff, and Howard Hogan. "An Aging Nation: The Older Population in the United States." United States Census Bureau, May 2014. https://www.census.gov/prod/2014pubs/p25-1140.pdf.

"Pay Equity and Discrimination." The Institute for Women's Policy, Research. Accessed October 30, 2018. https://iwpr.org/issue/employment-education-economic-change/pay-equity-discrimination/.

Redfoot, Donald, Lynn Feinberg, and Ari Houser. "The Aging of the Baby Boom and the Growing Care Gap: A Look at Future Declines in the Availability of Family Caregivers." AARP Public Policy Institute. https://www.aarp.org/content/dam/aarp/research/public_policy_institute/ltc/2013/baby-boom-and-the-growing-care-gap-insight-AARP-ppi-ltc.pdf.

Rosofsky, Ira, PhD. "Caregiver Stress: Would You Like Some Angst with That Sandwich Generation?" *Psychology Today*, April 12, 2009. https://www.psychologytoday.com/us/blog/adventures-in-old-age/200904/caregiver-stress-would-you-some-angst-sandwich-generation.

Roth, David L., PhD, Lisa Fredman, PhD, and William E. Haley. "Informal Caregiving and Its Impact on Health: A Reappraisal from Population-Based Studies." *The Gerontologist* 55, no. 2 (April 1, 2015): 309–19. https://doi.org/10.1093/geront/gnu177.

Span, Paula. "Caregiving's Hidden Benefits." *New York Times*, October 12, 2011. https://newoldage.blogs.nytimes.com/2011/10/12/caregivings-hidden-benefits/?mtrref=www.google.com.

"Work and Eldercare." Family Caregiver Alliance. Accessed October 30, 2018. https://www.caregiver.org/work-and-eldercare.

CHAPTER 3

Caring.com. "80% of Caregivers Report Strain on Their Marriages." February 5, 2009. https://www.caring.com/about/news-room/press-release-caregiver-marital-stress.

Centers for Disease Control and Prevention. "QuickStats: Percentage of Adults Who Often Felt Very Tired or Exhausted in the Past 3 Months,* by Sex and Age Group—National Health Interview Survey, United States, 2010–2011." April 12, 2013. https://www.cdc.gov/mmwr/preview/mmwrhtml/mm6214a5.htm.

Johnston, Katie. "Nearly 1 in 4 US Workers Go Without Paid Time Off." *Boston Globe*, August 14, 2014. https://www.bostonglobe.com/business/2014/08/13/one-few-countries-that-doesn-mandate-paid-vacation-time/eqodEqumohPyca5kt6hrZO/story.html.

National Alliance for Caregiving and AARP. "Caregiving in the U.S." June 2015. https://www.aarp.org/content/dam/aarp/ppi/2015/caregiving-in-the-united-states-2015-report-revised.pdf.

U.S. Bureau of Labor Statistics. "American Time Use Survey." Last modified December 20, 2016. https://www.bls.gov/tus/charts/household.htm.

————. "Volunteering in the United States, 2015." February 25, 2016. https://www.bls.gov/news.release/volun.nr0.htm.

CHAPTER 4

AfterEllen.com, The Linster. "Variations on Your Theme (Song)." July 14, 2008. https://www.afterellen.com/general-news/34691-variations-on-your-theme-song#3tdBe0lgoPhjRrDZ.99.

Baskin, Kara. "Female Executives Discuss How Motherhood Has Helped Them on the Job." *Boston Globe*, October 4, 2017. https://www.bostonglobe.com/magazine/2017/10/24/female-executives-discuss-how-motherhood-has-helped-them-job/EkT2i2aAVZaSpC1PqjZmyI/story.html.

Bernard, Tara Siegel. "The Unspoken Stigma of Workplace Flexibility." *New York Times*, June 4, 2013. https://www.nytimes.com/2013/06/15/your-money/the-unspoken-stigma-of-workplace-flexibility.html.

Casserly, Meghan. "Forbes Woman and TheBump.Com 'Parenthood and Economy 2012' Survey Results." *Forbes*, September 12, 2012. https://www.forbes.com/sites/meghancasserly/2012/09/12/forbeswoman-and-thebump-com-parenthood-and-economy-2012-survey-results/#313ed5c83212.

Deloitte. "Deloitte Announces 16 Weeks of Fully Paid Family Leave Time for Caregiving." September 8, 2016. https://www2.deloitte.com/us/en/pages/about-deloitte/articles/press-releases/deloitte-announces-sixteen-weeks-of-fully-paid-family-leave-time-for-caregiving.html.

Federal Reserve Bank of St. Louis. "Long-Term Unemployment Affected Older Women Most Following Recession." November 17, 2015. https://www.stlouisfed.org/on-the-economy/2015/november/older-women-recession-long-term-unemployment.

Flinn, Brenda. "Millennials: The Emerging Generation of Family Caregivers." *AARP*, May 22, 2018. https://www.aarp.org/ppi/info-2018/millennial-family-caregiving.html.

Ghilarducci, Teresa. "Why Women Over 50 Can't Find Jobs." *PBS*, January 14, 2016. https://www.pbs.org/newshour/economy/women-over-50-face-cant-find-jobs.

Jenkins, JoAnn. "Caregiving Costly to Family Caregivers." *AARP*, https://www.aarp.org/caregiving/financial-legal/info-2017/family-caregiving-costly-jj.html.

Mahadevan, Alex. "Women Are Leaving the Workforce at a Staggering Rate." *AOL*, August 23, 2017. https://www.aol.com/article/finance/2017/08/23/women-are-leaving-the-workforce-at-a-staggering-rate-heres-why/23159057/.

Martin, Emmie. "Here's How Much Money American Women Earn at Every Age." *CNBC*, September 12, 2017. https://www.cnbc.com/2017/09/12/heres-how-much-money-american-women-earn-at-every-age.html.

MetLife. "U.S. Business Loses from $17.1 Billion to $33.6 Billion Per Year in Productivity for Caregivers Who Take Time from Their Work Responsibilities; Online Calculator Available for Employers to Determine Costs." July 11, 2006. https://www.businesswire.com/news/home/20060711005250/en/U.S.-Business-Loses-17.1-Billion-33.6-Billion.

Pitts-Catsouphes, M., C. Matz-Costa, and E. Besen. "Age and Generations. Understanding Experiences in the Workplace." Research Highlight 6, The Sloan Center on Aging and Work, Boston College, March 2009. https://www.bc.edu/content/dam/files/research_sites/agingandwork/pdf/publications/RH06_Age_Generations.pdf.

Plumb, Emma. "Take 5: Stanford Economist Nicholas Bloom on the Business Case for Telecommuting." 1 Million for Work Flexibility, accessed October 30, 2018. https://www.workflexibility.org/take-five-stanford-economist-nicholas-bloom-business-case-telecommuting/.

Toossi, Mitra, and Teresa L. Morisi. "Women in the Workforce Before, During, and After the Great Recession." U.S. Bureau of Labor Statistics, July 2017. https://www.bls.gov/spotlight/2017/women-in-the-workforce-before-during-and-after-the-great-recession/pdf/women-in-the-workforce-before-during-and-after-the-great-recession.pdf.

Transamerica Center for Retirement Studies. "Striking Similarities and Disconcerting Disconnects: Employers, Workers and Retirement Security 18th Annual Transamerica Retirement

Survey." August 2018. https://www.transamericacenter.org/docs/default-source/retirement-survey-of-employers/tcrs2018_sr_employer-retirement-research.pdf.
U.S. Bureau of Labor Statistics. "93 Percent of Managers and 46 Percent of Service Workers Had Paid Sick Leave Benefits in March 2017." *TED: The Economics Daily*, August 2, 2017. https://www.bls.gov/opub/ted/2017/93-percent-of-managers-and-46-percent-of-service-wor kers-had-paid-sick-leave-benefits-in-march-2017.htm.
Vodafone. "Vodafone Global Survey Reveals Rapid Adoption of Flexible Working." February 8, 2016. https://www.vodafone.com/content/index/media/vodafone-group-releases/2016/ flexible-working-survey.html#.
Walmart. "Working at Walmart. Opportunities and Benefits." Accessed October 30, 2018. https://corporate.walmart.com/our-story/working-at-walmart.

CHAPTER 5

Centers for Disease Control and Prevention, National Center for Injury Prevention and Control. Web-Based Injury Statistics Query and Reporting System (WISQARS) [online]. Accessed August 5, 2016. https://www.cdc.gov/injury/wisqars/.
Jefferson, Robin Seaton. "New Survey Finds Adult Children Want Their Parents to Age at Home." *Forbes*, August 20, 2017. https://www.forbes.com/sites/robinseatonjefferson/2017/ 04/30/new-survey-finds-adult-children-want-their-parents-to-age-at-home/#15c72bffb44b.
The White House. "Presidential Proclamation—National Family Caregivers Month, 2016." October 31, 2016. https://obamawhitehouse.archives.gov/the-press-office/2016/10/31/ presidential-proclamation-national-family-caregivers-month-2016.

CHAPTER 6

Bouchal, Shelley Raffin, RN, PhD, Lillian Rallison, RN, PhD, Nancy J. Moules, RN, PhD, and Shane Sinclair, PhD. "Holding On and Letting Go: Families' Experiences of Anticipatory Mourning in Terminal Cancer." University of Calgary, March 10, 2015. https://doi.org/10. 1177/0030222815574700.
Busch, Mark. "How to Preplan Your Funeral." *Busch*, March 26, 2016. www.busch.com/blog/ how-to-preplan-your-funeral.
Dizikes, Peter. "3 Questions: Joseph Coughlin on Innovation for an Aging Population." *MIT News*, November 8, 2017. http://news.mit.edu/2017/3-questions-joseph-coughlin-innovation-aging-population-1108.
PwC. "Formal Cost of Long-Term Care Services: How Can Society Meet a Growing Need?" Accessed October 30, 2018. https://www.pwc.com/us/en/industries/insurance/library/long-term-care-services.html.
Samuel, Lawrence R., PhD. "Americans in General Are Uncomfortable Thinking About Death." *Psychology Today*, June 23, 2015.
U.S. Department of Veteran Affairs. "Veterans." Accessed October 30, 2018. https://www. benefits.va.gov/persona/veteran-elderly.asp.

CHAPTER 7

AARP. "New State Law to Help Family Caregivers." *AARP*, accessed October 30, 2018. https:/ /www.aarp.org/politics-society/advocacy/caregiving-advocacy/info-2014/aarp-creates-model-state-bill.html.
Christensen, Clayton M., Michael E. Raynor, and Rory McDonald. "What Is Disruptive Innovation?" *Harvard Business Review*, December 2015. https://hbr.org/2015/12/what-is-disruptive-innovation.

Gleckman, Howard. "A New Snapshot of America's 44 Million Family Caregivers: Who They Are and What They Do." *Forbes*, June 4, 2015. https://www.forbes.com/sites/ howardgleckman/2015/06/04/a-new-snapshot-of-americas-44-million-family-caregivers-who-they-are-and-what-they-do/#4907e3bf3ab2.

Hartmann, Heidi, PhD, Jeff Hayes, PhD, Rebecca Huber, Kelly Rolfes-Haase, and Jooyeoun Suh, PhD. "The Shifting Supply and Demand of Care Work: The Growing Role of People of Color and Immigrants." Institute for Women's Policy Research, June 27, 2018.

Rossen, L. M., M. J. K. Osterman, B. E. Hamilton, and J. A. Martin. "Quarterly Provisional Estimates for Selected Birth Indicators, 2016–Quarter 1, 2018." National Center for Health Statistics. National Vital Statistics System, Vital Statistics Rapid Release Program, 2018. https://www.cdc.gov/nchs/nvss/vsrr/natality-dashboard.htm.

U.S. Department of Labor Wage and Hour Division. "Fact Sheet #25: Home Health Care and the Companionship Services Exemption Under the Fair Labor Standards Act (FLSA)." September 2013. https://www.dol.gov/whd/regs/compliance/whdfs25.pdf.

Woetzel, Jonathan, Anu Madgavkar, Kweilin Ellingrud, Eric Labaye, Sandrine Devillard, Eric Kutcher, James Manyika, Richard Dobbs, and Mekala Krishnan. "How Advancing Women's Equality Can Add $12 Trillion to Global Growth." McKinsey Global Report, September 2015. https://www.mckinsey.com/featured-insights/employment-and-growth/how-advancing-womens-equality-can-add-12-trillion-to-global-growth.

CHAPTER 8

American Dental Association. "Federal Government, ADA Emphasize Importance of Flossing and Interdental Cleaners." August 4, 2016. https://www.ada.org/en/press-room/news-releases/2016-archive/august/statement-from-the-american-dental-association-about-inter-dental-cleaners.

Brady, Sinead. "Self-Care Can Make You More Successful at Work." *Image*, January 23, 2018. https://www.image.ie/business/self-care-can-make-successful-work.

Breus, Michael J., PhD. "Yoga Can Help with Insomnia." *Psychology Today*, October 4, 2012. https://www.psychologytoday.com/us/blog/sleep-newzzz/201210/yoga-can-help-insomnia.

Centers for Disease Control and Prevention, National Center for Injury Prevention and Control. Web-Based Injury Statistics Query and Reporting System (WISQARS) [online]. Accessed August 5, 2016. https://www.cdc.gov/injury/wisqars/.

"Cold Weather Fitness Guide." American Heart Association. Accessed October 30, 2018. https://www.heart.org/idc/groups/heart-public/@wcm/@fc/documents/downloadable/ucm_ 457235.pdf.

Davidson, R. J., J. Kabat-Zinn, J. Schumacher, M. Rosenkranz, D. Muller, S. F. Santorelli, F. Urbanowski, A. Harrington, K. Bonus, and J. F. Sheridan. "Alterations in Brain and Immune Function Produced by Mindfulness Meditation." *Psychosomatic Medicine*, 2003. https:// www.ncbi.nlm.nih.gov/pubmed/12883106.

"Dietary Reference Intakes: Water, Potassium, Sodium, Chloride, and Sulfate." The National Academies of Sciences, Engineering, Medicine, February 11, 2014. http://www. nationalacademies.org/hmd/Reports/2004/Dietary-Reference-Intakes-Water-Potassium-Sodium-Chloride-and-Sulfate.aspx.

Emmons, Robert. "Why Gratitude Is Good." *Greater Good Magazine*, Greater Good Science Center at UC Berkeley, November 16, 2010. https://greatergood.berkeley.edu/article/item/ why_gratitude_is_good.

"Fifteen Benefits of Drinking Water." *Medical News Today*, July 16, 2018. https://www. medicalnewstoday.com/articles/290814.php.

Fredericks, Kim. "Here's What You Need to Know About the Health Benefits of Chocolate." *Reader's Digest*, accessed October 30, 2018. https://www.rd.com/health/wellness/health-benefits-of-chocolate/.

Horn, Stacy. "Singing Changes Your Brain: Group Singing Has Been Scientifically Proven to Lower Stress, Relieve Anxiety, and Elevate Endorphins." *Time*, August 16, 2013. http:// ideas.time.com/2013/08/16/singing-changes-your-brain/.

"It's Official—Spending Time Outside Is Good for You." University of East Anglia, June 7, 2018. https://www.uea.ac.uk/about/-/it-s-official-spending-time-outside-is-good-for-you.

Kaimal, Girija, Kendra Ray, and Juan Muniz. "Reduction of Cortisol Levels and Participants' Responses Following Art Making." May 23, 2016. https://www.tandfonline.com/doi/full/10.1080/07421656.2016.1166832.

Lewis, Danny. "Feeling Down? Scientists Say Cooking and Baking Could Help You Feel Better." *Smithsonian Magazine*, November 29, 2016. https://www.smithsonianmag.com/smart-news/feeling-down-scientists-say-cooking-and-baking-may-help-you-feel-better-180961223/#JyQLW7SzTJ7Oku25.99.

Lorde, Audra. *A Burst of Light and Other Essays.* Ithaca, NY: Firebrand Books, 1988.

Mayo Clinic. "Exercise and Stress: Get Moving to Manage Stress." Accessed October 30, 2018. https://www.mayoclinic.org/healthy-lifestyle/stress-management/in-depth/exercise-and-stress/art-20044469.

———. "Massage Therapy." August 10, 2017. https://www.mayoclinic.org/tests-procedures/massage-therapy/about/pac-20384595.

———. "Support Groups: Make Connections, Get Help." June 26, 2018. https://www.mayoclinic.org/healthy-lifestyle/stress-management/in-depth/support-groups/art-20044655.

Moore, Kimberly Sena, PhD. "Why Listening to Music Makes Us Feel Good." *Psychology Today*, January 20, 2011. https://www.psychologytoday.com/us/blog/your-musical-self/201101/why-listening-music-makes-us-feel-good.

Murray, Bridget. "Writing to Heal." *American Psychological Association* 33, no. 6 (June 2002). https://www.apa.org/monitor/jun02/writing.aspx.

"Take A Nap! Change Your Life," Sara Mednick, accessed October 30, 2018, https://www.saramednick.com.

Thøgersen-Ntoumani, C., E. A. Loughren, F. E. Kinnafick, I. M. Taylor, J. L. Duda, and K. R. Fox. "Changes in Work Affect in Response to Lunchtime Walking in Previously Physically Inactive Employees: A Randomized Trial." *Scandinavian Journal of Medicine and Science in Sports*, December 2015. https://www.ncbi.nlm.nih.gov/pubmed/25559067.

Shakya, Holly B., and Nicholas A. Christakis. "A New, More Rigorous Study Confirms: The More You Use Facebook, the Worse You Feel." *Harvard Business Review*, April 10, 2017. https://hbr.org/2017/04/a-new-more-rigorous-study-confirms-the-more-you-use-facebook-the-worse-you-feel.

Stromback, M., M. Wiklund, E. S. Renberg, and E. B. Malmgren-Olsson. "Complex Symptomatology among Young Women Who Present with Stress-Related Problems." *Scandinavian Journal of Caring Sciences* 29, no. 2 (2015): 234–47.https://www.ncbi.nlm.nih.gov/pubmed/24953100.

Van Den Berg, Agnes E., and Mariëtte H. G. Custers. "Gardening Promotes Neuroendocrine and Affective Restoration from Stress." *Journal of Health Psychology*, June 3, 2010. http://journals.sagepub.com/doi/10.1177/1359105310365577.

CHAPTER 9

Eisenberg, Richard. "Sorry, Nobody Wants Your Parents' Stuff." *Next Avenue*, February 9, 2017. www.nextavenue.org.

iRelaunch. https://www.irelaunch.com.

ReBootAccel. https://rebootaccel.com.

CHAPTER 10

American Psychological Association. "Positive Aspects of Caregiving." May 2014. https://www.apa.org/pi/about/publications/caregivers/faq/positive-aspects.aspx.

Boyd, Evelyn M., and Ann W. Fales. "Reflective Learning Key to Learning from Experience." *Journal of Humanistic Psychology*, April 1, 1983. https://doi.org/10.1177/0022167883232011.

Brown, Stephanie L., Dylan M. Smith, Richard Schulz, Mohammed U. Kabeto, Peter A. Ubel, Michael Poulin, Jaehee Yi, Catherine Kim, and Kenneth M. Langa. "Caregiving Behavior Is Associated With Decreased Mortality Risk." *Psychological Science*, April 20, 2009. https://www.ncbi.nlm.nih.gov/pmc/articles/PMC2865652/.

Ephron, Nora, "'62 Addressed the Graduates in 1996." Wellesley College Commencement Archives, https://www.wellesley.edu/events/commencement/archives/1996commencement.

Hamby, Sherry, PhD. "Resilience and . . . 4 Benefits to Sharing Your Story." *Psychology Today*, September 3, 2013. https://www.psychologytoday.com/us/blog/the-web-violence/201309/resilience-and-4-benefits-sharing-your-story.

MacGill, Markus. "What Is the Link between Love and Oxytocin?" *Medical News Today*, September 4, 2017. https://www.medicalnewstoday.com/articles/275795.php.

Index